SEXISM
AND THE
WAR SYSTEM

SEXISM
AND THE
WAR SYSTEM

Betty A. Reardon

Foreword by Patricia Schroeder

TEACHERS
COLLEGE
PRESS

Teachers College, Columbia University
New York and London

Published by Teachers College Press, 1234 Amsterdam Avenue, New York, N.Y. 10027

Grateful acknowledgment is made to reprint excerpts from THE PSYCHOANALYSIS OF WAR by Franco Fornari. Copyright© 1974 by Doubleday & Company, Inc. Reprinted by permission of the publisher.

Library of Congress Cataloging in Publication Data

Reardon, Betty.
  Sexism and the war system.

  Bibliography: p.
  Includes index.
  1. Peace — Research. 2. Women and peace.
3. Sexism. I. Title.
JX1904.5.R43   1985   327.1'72'088042   85-12619

ISBN 0-8077-2770-9
ISBN 0-8077-2769-5 (pbk.)

Manufactured in the United States of America

90 89 88 87 86   3 4 5 6

For Esther Stine in love and remembrance

I am tired of being the blood, the earth and the scream. I address the storyteller and those who have passed the tale down, written it down, recited and believed it. Is that all? I ask the storyteller. Where am I then? Do I have to be Abel if I don't want to be Cain? Is there no other way?

Dorothee Sölle,
"Peace Needs Women" (1982)

CONTENTS

FOREWORD

ALTHOUGH THE AMERICAN ELECTORATE has yet to send a woman to the White House and the women's movement still struggles for full legal assurance of equality in the passage of the Equal Rights Amendment, both American politics and the world at large have been forever affected by feminist politics. And of one thing we can be sure: while the women's movement may continue to see its ups and downs, it is here to stay and is determined to effect changes in the world.

Some of those changes are clearly spelled out by *Sexism and the War System*. Women are not going to be satisfied with token appointments or cosmetic changes. The changes we seek are fundamental and far-reaching, and we will not give up in our struggle for them nor in our insistence that we can change our own lives and the world. We insist on our own equality because we believe that political and social equality are essential. And we believe that a world that denies equality to women makes it impossible for all who are currently deprived of their human rights to achieve them. *Sexism and the War System* makes the case for the centrality of women's rights to the total struggle for human rights. It invites readers to explore the links between the denial of women's rights, the continuation of the arms race, and the perpetuation of war — the ultimate form of violence. It challenges both feminists and peace advocates to examine their points of view more deeply and to find new strength in the common ground between their respective movements.

There is little likelihood that all feminists or all peace advocates will entirely agree with Betty Reardon's analysis. But there are none who will not find here some ideas to explore as they seek to achieve a better understanding of why the world continues to keep half its population in a subservient position to the other half while it moves ever closer to destroying itself. *Sexism and the War System* explores these questions and offers a reason to believe that the real hope for a better world lies in the growing, worldwide women's movement.

PATRICIA SCHROEDER
U.S. Representative,
Colorado

ACKNOWLEDGMENTS

THIS MONOGRAPH is the fruit of several years' reflection, many conversations, and the criticisms and comments of friends and colleagues who read earlier drafts. It is the beginning of what is intended to be deeper reflection and more systematic study, and, I hope, the initiation of new and extended conversations and exchanges. I welcome comments and suggestions for further inquiry and expressions of differences in interpretation from others who have thought about the connections between the oppression of women and war.

There is much more to be considered than has been included here, especially in feminist scholarship and most particularly in that which focuses on the issues of women and war. I'm sure that the consideration of recent and extremely relevant works, most of which appeared at the time that *Sexism and the War System* was completed in the fall of 1983, would have enriched the work. The approach, however, is more from the perspective of peace education and peace research, which I believe have much to gain from feminist scholarship. A few feminist peace researchers have begun to pursue this learning, and they are among those whose support, criticism, and suggestions have been invaluable in this attempt to expose and explore the links between militarism and sexism. My colleagues in the Women, Militarism, and Disarmament Study Group of the International Peace Research Association have my gratitude and will continue to have my support for their individual and our common inquiries into these questions. I celebrate the beginning of our particular link in the global chain of women applying their skills and their insights to the struggle for a truly just world peace.

A most essential element of the support system that made this beginning possible was UNESCO, a grant from which enabled the study group to hold its first consultation in Gyor, Hungary, in August 1983, a session at which portions of this manuscript were presented. That consultation was one of a number of exchanges in which the hunches that began these reflections were validated by others with similar concerns.

The monograph itself was initiated with the support and encouragement of the World Policy Institute (WPI) and the World Order Models Project (WOMP). Indeed, the idea for this publication developed in a conversation with the co-directors of WOMP, Saul Mendlovitz and Yoshikazu Sakamoto. My special thanks to them, not only for "seeing the connections," but also for their willingness to open our common field of world order studies to the criticisms made here. Thanks, too, are extended to Sherle Schwenninger for his patience and encouragement while months often slipped away from the manuscript to other tasks, and to Steve Maikowski of WPI and Lois Patton of Teachers College Press for arranging the joint WPI-TC Press publishing.

I am especially grateful to all those who read and commented on the first draft, for their criticism and suggestions and the time and care they contributed to helping me clarify the ideas expressed here. I hope I have not done too badly in incorporating their suggestions. Although I've tried to provide citations to those concepts and interpretations derived from them and others, I'm sure a good deal more of this work than is so noted is more the consequence of these exchanges and comments than of original thought.

My most particular thanks go to Esther Stine and Patrick Lee for the comments and suggestions that sharpened the central concepts. Esther's questioning of the aspects relating to enemies and victims and Pat's identification of the notion of reciprocal causality helped me to the stage of understanding reflected here.

My thanks, too, to all who share the vision of a world liberated from the violence of oppression and war for endowing all aspects of the common struggle with meaning and value of their own, distinct from but essential to our common goal. Peace in the struggle.

SEXISM
AND THE
WAR SYSTEM

Chapter 1

INTRODUCTION

THE FUNDAMENTAL PURPOSE of this monograph is to argue the need for an integration of feminist scholarship with peace research in order to overcome the inadequacies of each in their separate attempts to abolish respectively sexism and war. This argument is grounded in the contention that both phenomena depend on violence. It leads to the assertion that only by the application of a theory of reciprocal causation giving equal consideration to both the psychological and the structural causes of sexism and the war system can we gain a sufficient understanding of the problems and their interrelationship to enable us to transcend them. Transcendence is possible because our problems derive primarily from learned behaviors resulting from an interplay between psychological and structural factors. Learned behaviors are subject to change, and change is a question of choice.

Feminists and peace researchers are currently faced with what I argue is a crucial choice in the development of human knowledge and human society. Whether they choose (as I argue they should) to merge their perspectives, modes of inquiry, and strategies for action or to continue on their distinctly separate but significantly parallel paths can make a profound difference in both epistemology and politics — particularly the politics of transformation. Before such a merger can take place, however, peace researchers must recognize the legitimate claims of women to full participation in all human affairs, including peace research. Such recognition, and movement toward the merger of feminism and the peace movement, would be a fitting and perhaps salvational culmination to the International Women's Decade (1975–85).

Since the United Nations declaration of International Women's Year in 1975 and the consequent International Women's Decade, much lip service has been given to the relationship of women to three basic themes: equality, development, and peace — the interrelationships among them, and their significance to the future of the planet. While most of the "official" and organized concerns and efforts in the industrial world have focused on equality, and in the Third World on development, virtually no substantive consideration nor even lip service has been given in either region to the relationship between women's issues and peace. Indeed, a group of women from one Western country who participated in the Tribune (an unofficial, nongovernmental conference held at the same time as the official United Nations International Women's Year Conference in Mexico in 1975) reported that they had been advised not to discuss peace and disarmament issues because they were not relevant to women's issues. Recently, however, a growing minority of feminist peace researchers have turned their attention to this particular topic.

My reflections during these years have been related primarily to the actual and potential roles of women and women's movements in the process of structural transformation, which the world order movement — comprising scholars and activists seeking to end war and oppression — sees as fundamental to the achievement of peace. These reflections on the need for women's perspectives and participation in the transformational process have led me to recognize the common characteristics and manifestations of women's oppression and warfare. It is clear that interrelationships exist between contemporary militarization and other reactionary trends, including opposition to the women's struggle for equality. A few feminist peace researchers, in fact, have moved from disciplined speculation to serious substantive study regarding the causes of both sexism and the war system, their common characteristics, and the interrelationships between sexist oppression and militarization.[1] I have come to believe that the two problems not only are symbiotically related, but are twin manifestations of the same underlying cause. This requires that they be viewed as twin, not separate, problems. They should command simultaneous and equal attention from those fields of research, education, and political action that purport to be devoted to their abolition.

Some parts of this monograph will doubtless be redundant for those who are familiar with the growing body of thought and the limited but significant literature on women and war and/or on feminism and militarism. However, I feel it necessary to recapitulate some of these conclusions in order to demonstrate the fundamental symbiosis between sexism and the war system. I do this particularly for two audi-

---

1. The evolution of these ideas is outlined in a series of articles by Betty Reardon (1975–1983). Those not included in the References are: "Debating the future," *Network, 8* (May/June 1980); "Women and disarmament: Traditional values in a transnational world," in *Women's contribution to peace*, ed. S. McClean (New York: UNESCO, 1981); "Research agenda for a gender analysis of militarism and sexist repression," *International Peace Research Newsletter, 21* (February 1983).

ences who are, in fact, addressing this common problem and who I believe could form a significant collaboration for its resolution, namely feminist educators, researchers, and activists and their counterparts in the peace research and world order inquiry movements. I believe that a constructive collaboration between them can make a significant contribution to the abolition of war. I also intuitively believe that the merger of these movements is probably necessary for human survival. It is certainly required if we are to move to a new stage in the humanization of society.

Four main influences have led to the conclusions and opinions that will be outlined here. The original reflections and speculations were initiated by a thesis proposal by Irma Garcia Chafardet (1975) regarding the origins of aggression in the distortion that rigid sex role socialization imposes upon "authentic" male and female attributes, and the collateral effects of these distortions on child care and child development. Her initial conceptualization of authentic and distorted male and female attributes helped me to distinguish between what I now designate as positive and negative masculine and feminine values. The positive values derive from the authentic attributes and are those that are conducive to the full realization of the human potential in both individuals and society. The negative values derive from the distorted attributes and are those that stifle and crush portions of human and social development. They are the values that underlie stereotypes and rationalize discrimination and oppression. Our present social order, as will be more fully outlined here, is overly characterized by these negative values, both feminine and masculine. However, so heavy is the emphasis on the negative masculine values, and so little emphasis is given to the positive feminine values, that the qualifying adjective is not generally used throughout the text. Arguments in favor of feminine values are, therefore, only for the positive, and arguments against the masculine are only against the negative.

These initial reflections and speculations were disciplined by the perspectives and approaches of world order studies, particularly their illumination of the interrelationships between global issues and structural problems, and by the world order focus on the interdependence of such components of the world survival crisis as war, population and poverty, and ecological imbalance. The world order influence is most especially reflected in the value dimensions of these reflections, particularly the emphasis on social justice and economic equity.

Reflections on the common roots of sexism and the war system were reinforced by the work of Franco Fornari, an Italian psychiatrist. His theory that the origins of war reside in the human psyche and the corollary assertion that the abolition of war requires that every person must assume some individual responsibility for war (Fornari, 1974), gave scholarly validation to my basic hunches.

Finally, Jan Oberg (1981) has asserted that disarmament cannot be addressed without giving analytic attention to the symbiotic relationship between armaments and structural violence. This makes it impossible to separate analytically or politically the problems of militarization from those of poverty and oppression and provides a precedent and paradigm for consideration of the kind of relationship that exists between sexism and the war system.

The world order inquiry framework is used here because I believe it best serves the two central concerns from which this monograph derives: the need for a realization of the human rights of women and for women's perspectives in addressing public issues; and also, and primarily, an immediate and specific anxiety about the increasing potential for human annihilation inherent in the nuclear arms race. In this monograph I suggest some contributions that world order studies can make to the achievement of the goals of economic equity, political empowerment, and social equality for women, but, more significantly, I attempt to offer some insights into sexism as a major obstacle to halting the arms race and reversing the planetary trend toward militarization.

I share the opinion of a strongly convinced minority of feminists, world order scholars, peace researchers, and educators that the achievement of these two objectives is not possible unless the problems are addressed within the context of the policy issues and normative controversies raised by feminism. Scholars sharing this conviction (among them some distinguished men and, indeed, most women in the field), acknowledge the desirability if not the necessity of women's movements attending more to the issues of war, armaments, and militarization. The underlying assumption of this acknowledgment is that feminine values, which nurture life and acknowledge the need for transcending competition and violence, are needed to guide policy formation to avoid or abolish war. Another related feminist assertion is that, notwithstanding the behavior of certain female leaders, the mere presence in the political process of more women socialized to hold such values can have an ameliorating effect on the problems of war and violence (Brock-Utne, 1981; Reardon, 1975c). Interestingly, virtually the same assertion was made in a review of biological research on the hormonal basis of the tendency for more aggressive behavior in males than in females (Konner, 1982).

There has been no refutation of these assertions on the part of nonfeminist (some might even say antifeminist) world order scholars and peace researchers. On the contrary, lip service has been given to them, as well as to the three themes of the International Women's Decade. However, virtually no peace researchers or world order scholars, other than those few feminists in the field, have advocated the need consciously to conscript women into peace research and world order studies or to include feminist perspectives or feminist issues in the field. Most tend to view women's issues as secondary or collateral issues to the central concern of peace. Some still maintain that the subject is a distraction from the more important and core issues involved in the reversal of the arms race and militarization, and the abolition of war (Carroll, 1972). Some researchers openly and completely reject the oppression of women as having any relation to questions of war and peace. (What is said around coffee tables in research institutes often is more truly revealing than what is said around seminar tables. Informal professional conversations can expose the sexist bias usually denounced in formal discourse.) On the other hand, some feminists assert that sexism is the most pervasive and most fundamental problem of world order — indeed, of human social evolution — because it is a root cause of violence, especially socially sanctioned violence.

In this monograph I attempt to make the case that sexism and the war system are two interdependent manifestations of a common problem: social violence. That common problem, while it is exacerbated and played out in contemporary economic, political, and social structures, does not derive solely from structural causes. Rather, the problem originates in the very roots of the human psyche, and will not be fully resolved until the majority of the human family recognizes the need for all individuals to involve themselves in the transformational struggle. Fornari (1974) argues that as individuals we all bear some responsibility for war, and I would argue the same for sexism, the fundamental source of which lies within each of us. Social structures, economic and political processes, like architecture and other art forms, derive from images arising from the human imagination and the human experience. Although we are profoundly influenced psychologically and socially by the structures, it is ourselves who create and can change them. It is the successful pursuit of the inner struggle, which was called "head changing" in the 1960s, that I believe constitutes the central transformational task. In relation to that task, disarmament, even the abolition of war, is only a transitional stage toward the achievement of one component of the authentic transformation:

the exorcising of violence and coercive force as the main cohesion of society (Reardon, 1980).

The working assumptions that underlie the basic problems reviewed in this monograph arise from a series of hunches, intuitions, and insights. Although the dictionary does not make very fine distinctions between those three concepts, they are to me stages of what has been recognized as a feminine mode of thought development; and it is important for the purpose of this piece — the encouragement of a convergence between women's movements and the world order movement — to provide at least a brief overview statement of those assumptions especially relevant to that purpose.

The initial assumption is one that is becoming widely shared among peace educators. It is that the major obstacle to disarmament is not political but psychosocial; it is fear — the fear of being defenseless in the face of an attacker or an antagonist — that is almost universally manifest in both individuals and in societies. Various peace researchers also assert that the problems of war and sexism arise not from nature or from instinct, but rather from social conditioning and acquired psychological needs. Although social conditioning and learned behaviors are currently a subject of study by both peace researchers and peace educators, few have yet addressed the psychological needs that are met by both the war system and sexism. The works of Garcia Chafardet and Fornari are notable exceptions to this lack of attention to psychological needs, and lead to a consideration of the possibility that social and political institutions actually derive from inner constructs of the human psyche. Therefore, achieving radical institutional change, which probably the abolition of war and certainly the abolition of violence necessitates, will require comprehension of what those inner constructs are.

Because we have created our own sociocultural environment, understanding ourselves becomes a primary requirement for changing that environment. A better understanding of our own psychosocial reality and the conditions and experiences that produced it can lead us not only to the requisite knowledge but, even more significantly, it can offer us hope for positive change. Both sexism and the war system are culturally conditioned and therefore subject to change. As my Teachers College colleague Patrick Lee put it in comments on an earlier draft of this work:

> Socio-cultural conditioning runs as deep as biology but, unlike the latter, it *can* change in a relatively few generations. Biological change of any significance takes hundreds or even thousands of generations.

> It is because we are such deeply socio-cultural creatures (i.e., self-created) that socio-cultural and psychic qualities *appear* as hard as instinct and "nature." There is a difference between *deep* and *hard*. The former is fundamental, but in principle open to relatively rapid historical change; the latter is also fundamental but less open to change. (P. Lee, personal communication, 1983)

The profoundly sexist history of the human species indicates that the socially induced and prescribed separations and differences between the sexes are a very significant component of the inner psychic constructs. They may well be the psychic origins of war, sexism, and all structures of violence and oppression. Various feminists have pointed to the oppression of women by men as the first and most fundamental form of structural oppression. (See Reardon [1975c] for citations from unpublished papers by feminist anthropologists.) It is clear that for both boys and girls the first socially encountered other, a person they perceive as being different from themselves, is usually of the other sex; and our experience indicates that it is others, those different from us, who threaten us and instigate the fear that gives rise to the notion of enemy and, ultimately, the practice of war. Society reinforces and exacerbates this perception of otherness.

It is, I think, of some significance that psychiatry has pointed out that the enemy always becomes the embodiment of what we fear or reject in ourselves. We attempt to exorcize our own bad spirits by projecting them on others. A major function of others is, in fact, to meet various needs we cannot fulfill ourselves. When these needs are recognized as positive and good, we love or feel kindly toward the others who fulfill them. When they are negative or bad, we hate and despise the others and fear their power over us. For only by granting them such power can we abnegate responsibility for our own negative behavior. A classic case of this process is attributing temptress behavior to women who "lead men astray" and making the prostitute but not her client culpable before the law. We usually manage to punish others for our own sins. Society thus needs criminals and enemies. Eve was the first of many to serve "mankind." Because we have yet to learn the full wisdom of the popular sage Pogo ("We have met the enemy and he is us"), the enemy is always other, and feared. It is widely acknowledged that both sexist society and the war system are kept in order by the capacity to use or threaten the use of violence against those others who arouse fear.

It is important to note that various researchers have asserted that the similarities between males and females of the human species are far more significant and numerous than the differences (Lee & Gropper, 1974). In fact, in humans the similarities are stronger than in most other species. Lee and Gropper cite Birdwhistell's argument that the differences imposed by custom and socialization originated in the need to have visible signs of otherness for purposes of mating and reproduction, purposes served in other species by more readily perceivable signals.

Research does indicate that most of the behavioral differences between human males and females are the consequence of socialization and education. The artificial differentiation thus imposed on men and women leaves in its wake a very deep sense of fragmentation and loss, perhaps even a sense of having been wounded or traumatized by a rending of one set of characteristics from every human being at the time of birth—a cleavage that I refer to as the primal wound. A sense of trauma and pain can be one source of what has been identified as an instinctual fear of others and could possibly account for the presence of what has been designated as natural aggression. What is important here is to recognize the common emotional roots as well as the structural interrelationships between sexism and the war system. Both are grounded to a large extent in the primitive fear of the other. These commonalities must be taken into consideration by world order studies and schemes, particularly when such studies and schemes attempt to deal with transition to peace or with the requirements of transformation of the global social system.

These psychic areas of concern are not always taken into account in planning for structural change, but should be an integral part of the research and policy planning for what world order advocates call global transformation. In addition to the value changes advanced by world order advocates, some fundamental psychic transformations are required to change both those social processes and those human behaviors that are now primarily energized by violent force. World order scholars and advocates should recognize the importance of changes within individuals as necessary components of global transformation because a fundamental fear standing in the way of disarmament is fear in the individual person, projected onto the social order (Fornari, 1974).

In asserting the need for inner change, the intent is not to argue the irrelevance of sociopolitical determinants, but rather to observe their inadequacy to a truly transformation-oriented analysis. It certainly can be argued that the fears fueling the present arms race are "organized by human social structures" and "introjected into the individual psyche" (P. Lee, personal communication, 1983). The Sovietophobia in the United States and the fear of nuclear war in very young children bear witness to this. What peace research and world order studies need to be working toward is an understanding of the interplay between social structures and psychological forces, for "human sociality and human personality are reciprocally determining" (P. Lee, personal communication, 1983).

Finally, it must be recognized that transition as well as transformation will need to be learned, just as the conduct of warfare and the practice of sexism are learned. The transcendence of warfare and sexism at the behavioral level can also be learned. We can engage in a conscious learning process to change human relations and change the world political system. However, the quality of those changes will depend in large part on how we address the "war within" — the struggle created in every human being by the cleaving of the total human potential and personality into two distinct and separate parts, male and female, which are molded into socially rigid and confining sex roles.

Chapter 2

CORE CONCEPTS, BASIC ASSUMPTIONS, AND FUNDAMENTAL VALUES

THE PROBLEMS AND ISSUES to be explored in this examination of sexism and the war system are viewed through four major conceptual lenses: the war system, sexism, feminism, and world order. Each concept comprises a set of subconcepts and the underlying assumptions that determine the connotations carried by the conceptual terms. I offer the following definitions not as an assertion of the essential meaning of the concepts but rather to clarify the terms as they are used in this work. They are offered as well to expose my own underlying assumptions and to support the thesis that the two phenomena, sexism and the war system, arise from the same set of authoritarian constructs. I put them forth in an effort to encourage further reflection on the meanings of these terms, which are widely used in discussions about peace and feminism — subjects about which there is little conceptual clarity.

The War System:
Enforcement of Patriarchy

My use of the term *war system* refers to our competitive social order, which is based on authoritarian principles, assumes unequal value among and between human beings, and is held in place by coercive force. The institutions through which this force is currently controlled and applied are dominated by a small minority, elites who run the global economy and conduct the affairs of state. These elites are men from industrial countries, primarily Western, and for the most part educated to think in Western, analytic terms. Although their relationship is competitive within the elite structures, there is a common objective that holds the elites together: the maintenance of their own control and dominance. This purpose accounts for the degree of accommodation and cooperation that can be found among all elites. Their primary competition is therefore with the nonelites, the majority of the world's people. Control is maintained by force in the form of threat, intimidation, and, when necessary, violent coercion. The control system requires that only intimidation and threat of force be used whenever possible, in part to save the cost of violent coercion but mainly to keep the majority at a sufficient level of well-being to maintain their productive capacity.

This latter, fundamental purpose of maintaining productive capacity necessitates a level of subelites within the general hierarchical structure. These subelites, for example, heads of client states, military officers, or favorite wives, carry out the day-to-day management of the productive functions of the majority of the population. Their lot is sufficiently better than the majority, from whose ranks they are usually drawn, to convince them that service to the elites and maintenance of the system is in their own best interest. They help keep the basic conflict between the elites and the majority submerged in cultural norms, traditional myths, and political ideologies. Their effectiveness depends on their remaining as removed as possible from the actual application of force, which is executed by more replaceable individuals. With the exception of those states so militarized that state violence need not be obscured, a general characteristic of the system is that the higher the level of command, the farther away it is from the actual application of violent force or the conduct of warfare. Like Persian emperors of ancient times, who surveyed combat from a hill miles away from the actual battle, today's imperial commanders of the nuclear era can take to an aircraft or special underground complexes.

The war system pervades our lives and affects every aspect of society from the structural to the interpersonal. It depends on the willingness of the majority to support the system, if not out of fundamental belief (nurtured by ideology and bolstered by rewards such as the material advantages that come to the winning side) then out of fear, preferably of a threat from outside the social unit controlled by a particular elite. But if crisis or threat to the established order calls for it, fear of the source of control, the elites themselves, is often engendered. As the units of control grow larger, there is more need to demonstrate the ability to overcome competitors, to deter them, and if necessary to take from them resources that may be needed to keep the majority at the level of well-being that will assure its continued support of the system. Continued support also is maintained by keeping the majority ignorant of their own interests and isolated from each other, and by encouraging a sense of competition to achieve the benefits that can be provided only by the elites. When this support is in jeopardy the elites must convince the majority that there is an outside threat more detrimental to the common good than their authority. Otherwise they must increase their power to intimidate, or even use coercion and violence to keep the populace in line. Thus the system throughout its history has continued to devote significant efforts and ever larger quantities of resources to war and the capacity to conduct warfare. I believe that the system produced war, not that war produced the system. Authoritarian patriarchy, which seems to have emerged with the major elements of "civilization"—human settlements, organized agriculture, the state, and male domination—invented and maintains war to hold in place the social order it spawned (Anonymous, 1967).

That this system or, in Fornari's phrase, social institution, has profound psychological roots and serves particular emotional needs is reflected in his concept of the "Terrifier." To me this notion seems to complement the idea of a sense of trauma from a severe psychic wound inflicted by the severance of human potentiality into distinct male and female categories. Fornari says of war:

> This organization serves two security functions and may be pictured as an iceberg, one part of which is visible and the other hidden in deep waters. The first part corresponds to the defense against external danger (i.e., the real flesh-and-blood enemy), while the other, the hidden part, corresponds to an unconscious security maneuver against terrifying fantasy entities which are not flesh and blood but represent an absolute danger (as experienced, for example, in nightmares) which we could call the "Terrifier."
>
> If we remain on the purely politico-military level, i.e., on the external part of the iceberg, the most obvious and generally held opinion is that war protects us from enemies who threaten our security, that is to say, from *external aggressors*.
>
> If, however, we employ the psychoanalytic instrument of investigation, the instrument invented specifically for the exploration of the unconscious, we find that the submerged part of the iceberg—the invisible part of war as a security organization—serves to defend ourselves against the "Terrifier" as an internal, absolute enemy similar to a nightmare, through *a maneuver which transforms this terrifying but ultimately unaffrontable and invulnerable entity into an external, flesh-and-blood adversary who can be faced and killed*. If we now pause to reflect on the singular relation between these two systems of security that are coinvolved in war, we arrive at the paradoxical conclusion that *war is a security organization not because it permits us to*

defend ourselves from real enemies, but because it succeeds in finding, or in extreme cases, in inventing, real enemies to kill; and that if it were not for war, society would be apt to leave men defenseless before the emergence of the Terrifier as a purely internal foe. (As we shall see later, this did happen in the case of the Kanachi tribes.)

In this manner we arrive at the incredible paradox that the most important security function is not to defend ourselves from an external enemy, but *to find a real enemy.* (Fornari, 1974, pp. xvi–xvii. Italics in original.)

The subconcepts of the war system relevant to this discussion are war, warfare, militarism, and militarization. *War*—a legally sanctioned, institutionally organized armed force, applied by authority to maintain social control, pursue public objectives, protect vital interests, and resolve conflicts—is grounded in the assumption that coercive force is the ultimate and the most effective mechanism for obtaining and maintaining these desired conditions. It does not necessarily exclude alternatives, but all other approaches are viewed as second best in effectiveness. The "security" of the state depends on its ability to wage war. War has, therefore, been legitimated and institutionalized. It has been a constant factor in the evolution of social and economic structures, subject to regulation and guaranteed citizen support by law, enshrined in religious tradition, rationalized by theology, aided by science, and developed into the psychological paradigm through which we view much of the entire human experience. Most significantly, its use has been the exclusive prerogative—indeed, the sacred precinct—of the political elites, a privilege recognized by international law and sanctified by religion. Patriarchy has nourished its central belief system by reserving solely as the right of the male elites (with a few minor and some mythical exceptions) the waging of war, the making of law, and mediating between humankind and the divine. The contemporary feminist challenge to these bastions—the armed forces, the government, and the church—is no less heretical (heresy, of course, as defined and judged by the male elites) and world shaking then were the assertions of Copernicus.

Warfare—the agglomeration of the skills, arts, and sciences of carrying out war—carries with it an assumption that the means and mechanisms of using armed force must be systematized and continually made more effective. Science has always served warfare, and technology has been profoundly influenced by it. In our age the lion's share of scientific research and technological development goes into war-making capacity and refining the techniques of warfare. Science and technology also have been fields traditionally closed to women, and some argue that this exclusion has influenced the objectives these fields have served (Chilchinisky, 1978).

The excessive pursuit of a more effective means of waging war frequently leads to the emergence of a warfare state. This is true especially when a society places continually greater emphasis on and accords increasing value and resources to having a greater war-making capacity than any of its actual or potential opponents. The current escalating arms race is an example of such an emphasis. It has turned the United States, the Soviet Union, and numerous other nations into warfare states.

Militarism — the belief system that upholds the legitimacy of military control of the state — is based on the assumption that military values and policies are conducive to a secure and orderly society. It has served to legitimate both warfare and civil use of coercive force (i.e., national guards and militia) in the interest of "national security." It is not surprising, given the relationship between patriarchy and the war system, that the more militarist a society tends to be the more sexist are its institutions and values. Feminists have noted this relationship in such cases as Nazi Germany and, more recently, Chile.

Militarization — the process of emphasizing military values, policies, and preparedness, often transferring civil functions to military authority — assumes that when a society is in crisis or threatened, the crisis or threat can best be weathered by strengthening the military. Two significant indicators of militarization are public expenditures, particularly the percentage of total expenditures allocated to military purposes, and the discussion or application of military measures as solutions to problems and conflicts that are basically political or economic. It should be noted that women take virtually no part in the decision making regarding such policies and that increasing military spending at the cost of social expenditures impacts most negatively on women (Kelber, 1982). It contributes significantly to the feminization of poverty. Sivard (1982) indicates that the majority of the world's poor will soon be women.

The militarization of post-World War II Euro-American society has paralleled the women's movement. Given the chronological relationship of the two phenomena and some of the working assumptions shared by feminists and the peace movement, this relationship is likely to be more than coincidental. It was to be expected that Phyllis Schlafly, heroine of the New Right, would take on the nuclear freeze movement in the wake of the defeat of the Equal Rights Amendment. Much of contemporary feminism that is anathema to the New Right springs from conceptual roots totally antithetical to the concepts of war, warfare, militarism, and militarization, which derive from negative masculine values. Militarism manifests the excesses of those characteristics generally referred to as *machismo*, a term that originally connoted the strength, bravery, and responsibility necessary to fulfill male social functions (Reardon, 1981, pp. 6–10). Militarist concepts and values are upheld by patriarchy, the structures and practices of which have been embodied in the state, forming the basic paradigm for the nation-state system. Thus there is in all aspects of that system an inevitable sexist bias that is especially acute in matters related to security, the term all political units apply to self-preservation. Security is the impulse that produces the *military* — "structures of organized violence controlled by the state" (Enloe, 1981).

Thus patriarchy is the central core of the conceptual structure that determines virtually all human enterprise, both public and private:

> Patriarchy is a set of beliefs and values supported by institutions and backed by the threat of violence. It lays down the supposedly "proper" relations between *men and women*, between *women* and *women* and between *men* and *men*. It imposes structures which make some work "naturally" men's work and other work "naturally" women's work. And it gives whatever is men's work more value, more significance, more pay. Patriarchy tries to divide women among themselves by asserting that each woman should see her greatest loyalty, protection and self-identification lodged in her relationship to a man. . . .
>
> Finally, patriarchy is a destructive structure for defining "proper" relations between men themselves. Men in most societies are taught very early to be "masculine," to respect only other men who are "masculine," to compete with each other, to use women to create modes of exchange with each other, to hide their fears and compassion from one another, to treat their sons differently than they treat their daughters. All of these dimensions of patriarchy — its assumptions, its values, its divisions of labour — are crystallized and hardened in the military, the most patriarchal institution in an already patriarchical society. (Elster, 1981)

The military, then, is the distilled embodiment of patriarchy; the militarization of society is the unchecked manifestation of patriarchy as the *overt* and *explicit* mode of governance.

Sexism and Feminism:
The System in Crisis

Sexism is a many-headed, ubiquitous monster that has manifested itself in different ways in different historic periods and in different cultures. It is a belief system based on the assumption that the physical differences between males and females are so significant that they should determine virtually all social and economic roles of men and women. It holds that not just their reproductive functions are determined by sex, but that sex is the factor that rules their entire lives, all their functions in society and the economy, and their relation to the state and all public institutions and especially to each other. Sexism is manifest in all forms of behavior from subtle gestures and language to exploitation and oppression, and in all human institutions from the family to the multinational corporation. It is as complex and pervasive a phenomenon as is the war system. Few human beings escape the social conditioning of both, and only a small minority have transcended them.

The major attitudinal underpinning of sexism lies in the belief that men are biologically and intellectually superior to women. This belief gives rise to those behaviors designated as *male chauvinism* — discrimination against women comprising the obvious and generally accepted social, economic, and political customs and practices and the legal institutions that legitimate and maintain the subordination of women. Male chauvinism operates in all spheres of private and public life, from women being subject to fathers, husbands, and even to sons, and to job discrimination and exclusion from the realms of power, particularly technology and politics. At one point in the women's movement male chauvinism was viewed as the core as well as the major manifestation of sexism. The terms were used synonymously. However, continued research and reflection make it clear that sexism is far more complicated and more deeply rooted than such visible and obvious aspects as chauvinist behavior, or even economic and political discrimination against women.

In fact, male chauvinism has served the women's movement as pain serves the body — as a warning of disease or dysfunction. It has been the target of much of the social and legal reform enacted in the interest of women's rights. Virtually all societies have come to condemn and to invoke laws against overtly misogynous behaviors such as suttee, be it the religiously based version practiced in Asia or the socioeconomic version practiced against widows and divorcees in Europe and the United States. The organized political efforts of the women's movement, while having had little discernible effect on underlying attitudes, have resulted at least in general statements of principle such as the U.N. declarations and some legal prohibitions of discrimination.

Attempts to overcome the discriminatory practices resulting from male chauvinism have given rise to sex-related directives in fair employment practice guidelines, sex equity in education programs, and equal rights legislation, which have represented the political objectives of the women's movement in the First World. In the Third World such attempts have taken the form of programs to include women in the development process. While such measures attempt to stamp out exclusion as a major form of discrimination, none has satisfactorily addressed the misogyny and gynophobia that underlie the discriminatory practices. Fear and hatred of one who has held total power over you is almost inevitable. Probably the most universal embodiment of total power is that of the mother over the young child. The love/hate/fear/dependence relationship that hostages frequently develop with their captors is not dissimilar to an attitude many feminists and some psychologists suspect most human beings harbor toward women (Chodorow, 1978). Efforts to prevent a recurrence of such thralldom are made as a common response to the experience of being subject to the total control of another. "Don't become vulnerable to a potential captor/tyrant, be it a militant student or a mother," we respond. "Keep those who have such potential away from opportunities to exploit it. If we let women into places of power and influence they may enslave us again as they did when we depended totally on their bodies for our physical survival, on their love for our identity, and on their approval for our self worth."

That fear produces hatred is a phenomenon documented by psychological research and acknowledged by common sense. A two-year-old seized by a tantrum, screaming "I hate you" at her mother, and an enraged husband beating his wife may well be giving vent to the same primal feelings. Misogyny and gynophobia are destructive but understandable causes of male chauvinism in both men and women. All of us have had this experience of thralldom, the powerlessness of dependent childhood, and cannot be expected to be immune to the male chauvinist form of sexism.

Even when the experience of primary parenting is not with a woman, individuals are still as much subject to the general social resentment of mothers as they are to the sentimentalization of motherhood. Popular sentiment projects ideal images beyond the capacities of most women, setting them up for resentment by their offspring, who feel their mothers have failed them. All this occurs even in those disadvantaged sectors of society who never heard of Freud or of those theories of pop psychology that blame mothers for our emotional problems.

Perhaps we may hope for change in these socially communicated attitudes as a consequence of the varied new patterns of parenting. To date no research or systematic observation has been conducted on the development of children who are being mothered by fathers, although doubtless thousands of children have, in fact, been reared from birth by men. What difference this produces in the psychological profile of such children has not been explored. Certainly more and more children are now being cared for by fathers as well as mothers, and so grown up less totally dependent on a woman. The opportunity to make some systematic observations of this type of child rearing now exists, providing us with an opportunity to inquire more fully into the relationship between mothering, sexism, and aggression.

We cannot leave the topic of parenting without observing that it is our experience with those who parent us that probably determines how we view ourselves and forms our attitudes toward the world. Love and care also are learned. Although the emotional connection between the status of women and war is acknowledged more than that between sexism and the war system, male chauvinist attitudes sentimentalize and trivialize the connection, obscuring its real significance to the continuation of generations of violence and sexist repression.

Male chauvinism also has influenced concepts of what is masculine and what is feminine and, indeed, serves to define "man" and "woman," for men and women are socially perceived as exercisers of sex roles and as individuals characterized by masculine and feminine attributes. A "real man" demonstrates a full complement of masculine attributes, and a "real woman" demonstrates the complement of feminine attributes. These attributes are socially defined. Very few are based on physical characteristics; those that are are based primarily on secondary sexual characteristics. A man with very strong musculature may be considered to be more masculine than one of slight build, and a woman with a particularly curvacious figure may be considered to be more feminine than a thin one. However, the attributes of masculinity and femininity that are believed to be truly significant are behavioral and relate to such things as aggressive, assertive, masculine behavior or accommodating, dependent feminine behavior.

It is not especially relevant here to rehearse the range of characteristics that define masculinity and femininity. It is important, however, to emphasize that the imposition of different forms of behavior on men and women reinforces several characteristics of the war system. The next section explores these reinforcements. Probably the two most serious are the permission that most societies give to men to indulge aggressive impulses while prohibiting these impulses in women, and the encouragement of men to be competitive, even to the point of using violence to achieve success, while discouraging competitiveness in women. An exception, of course, is encouragement of competition among women to "win" and "hold on to" a man. Men also are permitted to exercise and act out anger, whereas women are expected to suppress it. A whole panoply of behaviors that encourage, even sanction, violence as a manifestation of masculinity and male identity have been designated as commendable, even virtuous public behaviors; the "stuff of greatness"; a profound influence on our total social ethos.

Although the connection may be less obvious, feminine characteristics, particularly the negative ones, also can be seen as reinforcing the war system: dependence and submission are acceptable and necessary behaviors in certain human beings. Oberg (1981) offers a thesis regarding the need to acknowledge the relationship between war and the arms race and the institutional violence of economic exploitation, that is, the dependence-dominance factors in the world economic system. This basic dependence-dominance behavior in male-female relations can be viewed as a reinforcing factor in the maintenance of the war system.[2]

Although a certain division of tasks based on sexual characteristics is necessary for child bearing, infant nurturance, and probably for certain survival processes in pretechnological societies, in contemporary industrial society sex-role differentiation for economic and political purposes is obsolete and increasingly recognized to be so (although gender inequalities remain). The social and psychological differences, however, even in technological society, are still assumed to be the consequence of nature and not subject to planned change or to conscious modification of behavior. Thus, although "men's jobs" and "women's jobs" are no longer advertised as such, and women are sometimes actively recruited for employment previously considered as exclusively within the male preserve, most men and women are still bound into rigidly defined social behaviors and psychological expectations that the culture designates as sex related. Most importantly, these behaviors and expectations are perceived as necessary for order, security, or the defense of national interests.

---

2. The social and behavioral distinctions between masculine-feminine and male-female are explored in detail in two previously cited articles by Reardon (1980, 1981).

That the culture perpetuates violence is a problem recognized by most peace researchers. That the culture also cultivates aggression by frustrating the total human potential through the imposition of rigidly defined sex roles, and the relationship of that imposition to socially sanctioned violence, have yet to be fully recognized. It is this imposition, as it affects both men and women, that constitutes the true problem of sexism.

Sexism — the imposition of a specific sex-related identity, a sexually determined set of human attributes, and sex-prescribed social roles — therefore reduces the significance of nongender criteria in the self-development and definition of all human beings. So viewed, sexism is equally damaging to both sexes, poses a severe obstacle to the development of a more synthesized and humane social order, and serves as a contributing factor in the maintenance of both the organized violence of warfare and the structural violence of economic exploitation, political oppression, and social discrimination.

Feminism is a response to this problem, particularly as it is manifested in male chauvinism. The intellectual and political roots of contemporary feminism are found in the Enlightenment, which produced the origins of modern political thought and our modern concepts of equality and universal human rights. Feminism is a strand of the human rights movement that insists on women's equality in the most fundamental and fullest sense of the word. *Feminism* is the belief that women are of equal social and human value with men, and that the differences between men and women, whether biologically based or culturally derived, do not and should not constitute grounds for discrimination against women. Feminists both male and female assert that women are fully human persons and should so be treated, as a group and individually. Feminists also insist that women need not adopt or manifest masculine values and behaviors to assert equality, nor do they devalue feminine characteristics, values, and capacities. These are viewed as an important component of the full range of human capacities, those society has chosen to develop in women and let atrophy in men. They seek to introduce feminine values into the social and political realms from which they have been excluded. The achievement of this end, it is recognized but seldom openly articulated, would constitute a profound social transformation.

Contemporary feminism is a global but highly varied phenomenon. In fact, it cannot be said that there is one general feminist or women's movement, for there are as many different women's movements as there are differing conditions and circumstances of oppression and discrimination against women. All women's movements are not feminist movements. Indeed, the concept of feminism may have raised more controversy within women's groups than in society at large. It should be observed, however, that had feminist endeavors been taken more seriously, even in the first stages of the contemporary phase, the profound and fundamental issues being raised would have produced even more controversy. Only in the case of specific legislative efforts or certain types of affirmative action has opposition to women's rights been publicly organized and articulated. For the most part, efforts to overcome sexual discrimination have been ignored, ridiculed, or countered with ploys of the "sexist conspiracy" so subtle, so ancient, so deep and quiet that they frequently go unnoticed. The silence is seldom broken except when feminism presents its positions and goals as feminist, or under the banner of women's liberation. Of the various subconcepts that constitute the central concept of feminism, these two are perceived as connoting the deepest radicalism and being the most dangerous to the established order.

Women's liberation — the public manifestation of contemporary feminism — calls for freeing women from the discrimination of social and economic structures that imprison them in perpetual inferiority to men and exclude them from the public sector and the exercise of political and economic power. As its adherents concentrate on such issues as equal pay and publicly provided services such as child care, women's liberation threatens to deprive society of the unpaid labor of women, without which society in its present form could not function. The specter of threats to the purse and to traditional definitions of masculinity and femininity that is raised by the terms feminist and women's lib provokes a severe backlash from true male chauvinists, both male and female.

Women's liberation in its forays into the public sector and professional establishments has been essentially a Western movement, most active in the United States and Europe. Although it has borrowed its terminology and some of its strategies from oppressed minorities and colonial peoples struggling against racism and traditional imperialism, it still has little cultural or political relevance to the Third World in terms of tactics and specific issues. In fact, its consequences could be detrimental to Third World women through a struggle for economic equality for women of the overprivileged sectors in a grossly inequitable global economy.

Equity and equality for women are the basic and fundamental goals of feminism and women's liberation, and to some degree of all women's movements. Women's movements are, in simplest terms, women organized for the achievement of commonly held goals. Some of these goals are primarily for the benefit of women, but equally as many are for the general benefit of society or for oppressed groups, including both men and women. Women's organizations that deal with politics and social change tend to work for the latter type of goal. Indeed, some women's organizations have been badly shaken by conflicts and controversy over women's liberation and feminism when (mainly younger) members have insisted that sexist oppression should be as great a concern as the economic and political oppression of the poor, racial minorities, and developing nations. Such organizations and women's movements exist throughout the world and, although not generally feminist, are working for what they believe to be a more humane society — a society governed more by the principles of equality and equity than by exploitation and oppression.

Women's rights traditionally connotes the basic rights of citizenship and the special entitlements that should be provided to women largely because of their reproductive functions, mothering roles, and "physical weakness." The household maintenance and bearing and nurturing of children are seen as the primary functions of women, but women also have been accorded the right to work, essentially meaning the right to enter the labor force of the formal economic structures. This concept of work, contrary to the claims and struggles of the nineteenth-century movement to establish the field of home economics, assumes that the bearing and nurturing of children and household care are not work. It also assumes that this "nonwork" makes no valuable contribution to the formal economy and always will be primarily the responsibility of women, to be performed without remuneration (Land, 1982). Therefore, if women wish to exercise their right to work (outside the home) or their right to participate in the political process, they need some special protections. Women's rights advocates thus centered on such things as paid maternity leave, sometimes for periods up to six months or a year, assuming that no one other than the mother can care for an infant. This hard-dying assumption is reaffirmed in unsuccessful suits for paternity leave. It also demonstrates the basic misogyny of the attitude that breast-feeding and child nurturing are purely private functions, not appropriate in the work place or public spheres. Also included in these women's rights were certain job-related protections, such as prohibiting women from certain forms of manual work or from work during night hours when traveling to and from their jobs might leave them vulnerable to attack by predatory men. That some of these protections perpetuate the inequality of women has been noted elsewhere. They are no more than cosmetic changes in the basic exploitative system.

Women's rights have also included the franchise, the right to seek and hold office, and the full range of traditional Western political rights. Whereas the women's suffrage movement conceived of these rights as fundamental and universal entitlements of all human beings, male-dominated society construed and granted them within the constraints of women's special and primary responsibility as mothers and housewives. Thus even the concept of women's rights became another way of separating women from the rest of humanity and from the "fully human" male membership of the human species rather than serving to illuminate a general problem of human rights. However, even for feminists who prefer not to separate women's rights from human rights, it often has been necessary to make a special case for women political prisoners subject to a more brutal treatment unique to their sex, because their cases get less attention than those of male prisoners.

This is a further illumination of the way in which women's issues are separated from general human issues even in the sphere of what are conceived as universal problems such as human rights. Granted, these special protections are an attempt to compensate for the exclusionary processes of politics and society and for historical inequities. Nevertheless, although they are intended to cushion the vulnerability that patriarchy has imposed on women, in recent years they have been used to perpetuate that vulnerability. One of the major arguments against such legislation as the Equal Rights Amendment is that the new law would abrogate women's special protections. A mainstay of patriarchy is, in fact, these special protections. Much as arms control measures serve to maintain the arms race by putting off substantive disarmament, special protections help to perpetuate the vulnerability and exploitability of women and children.

If we were to eliminate this innocent and protected category of humanity, the weak and powerless, by guaranteeing them their fundamental rights and endowing them with the collateral responsibilities (that is, empowering them), an important rationale for the superordinate emphasis on the defense system would be lost to the male power structure. The patriarchal state in negotiating the social contract has taken exclusive right to the use of force (coercive power) in return for defending a society that has rendered itself defenseless (given up the capacity to resist coercion) in return for the protection of the state. Members of the society no longer control their own security. These matters are handed over to the state and for the most part are subject to little review or question. While the benefits of this form of "disarmament" are apparent in the historic reduction of armed conflict within states, it has not contributed to reduction of armed conflict between states. On the contrary, it has increased the likelihood and the severity of international violence, as defense forces have been steadily increasing. Civil populations are now so heavily defended that they stand in jeopardy of annihilation. And the cost of this defense, as noted, is paid by the innocent, the truly defenseless — the poor and the weak, women, children, and the aged.

These special protections also serve to prevent the recognition of women's rights as women's entitlement to the basic universal human rights and serve through this separation mechanism to continue to isolate women's issues from the central fundamental concepts of politics and the social order. This separation also represents a significant barrier, not only to women's participation in global transformation, but to the achievement of global transformation. Separation and exclusion are particularly acute symptoms of the fundamental problem of sexism and thereby, as we shall see, contribute to the continuation of the war system. However, the links that connect human rights, exclusion, sexism, and the war system remain obscure and unexplored.

While feminism, particularly radical feminism, tends to address the more fundamental issues, even feminism has yet to deal fully with sexism at its deepest roots and in all its manifestations. Some feminists have begun to insist that women's problems be viewed as human rights issues. Certain factions of feminism have focused on the negative effects sexism imposes on both men and women. They see as their purpose the freeing of all human beings from these limitations. Yet feminism, even some of the more broadly construed aspects of the movement, is concerned primarily with bringing women's participation and perspectives into the spheres of politics, intellectual activities, the economy, and society in general.

As with other oppressed groups, many women have come to a stage at which they perceive their own interests as distinct from those of the dominant group. I believe that the prolongation of that stage is a potentially destructive fixation, one that could impede significant social change, but it is an understandable fixation given the way in which the fortunes of the women's movement wax and wane. Concentration on issues of equity for women is indeed defensible, especially considering that those fields of endeavor that purport to be struggling toward a more humane society (the peace movement, world order studies, peace research, and human rights campaigns) have focused little attention on women's oppression. Feminists, especially professional women and scientists who see the need to go beyond this stage, sometimes find it difficult to accept and indeed to work within an environment tainted by the antifeminist and antifeminine, antifemale attitudes found in these professions, as in all society.

It must be acknowledged, too, that there is an antimale attitude among some women who think of themselves as feminists. At its most negative this attitude is similar to what has been called reverse racism. This is especially true if it continues to focus attention and strategy on the separation of women's lives and interests from those of men, further fragmenting a conflict-ridden society by exposing only the surface levels of the conflict. This antimale attitude, based on the belief that men are the agents, if not the sole originators, of women's oppression, is as understandable as is the misogyny that grows from the total dependence of infants on women. Indeed, this anger and resentment has been as significant in the development of the feminist consciousness as the rejection of the mother has been in the development of children. Neither phenomenon should be accepted as any more inevitable than the conditions that produce them. Both must be confronted if we are to root out sexism and the aggression it fosters. The anger women feel has to be understood and met with something other than overt repression or by social norms that force the oppressed to turn their anger inward.

Another form of negative feminism is, in my opinion, that which accedes to the masculinization of women largely in attempts to prove that women can perform most tasks society reserves for men. Often, "doing the job as well as a man" means accepting masculine standards and thus reinforcing the dominant masculine values. This, I assert, offers new support for the war system. Such efforts to meet masculine, competitive, aggressive criteria of success narrow the possibilities for questioning the standards and changing the systems that are opened by women's entry into the man's world, the public sphere. They provide occasion for the co-optation of the women's movement into the very masculinization process that feeds militarism and impels the arms race. By making it possible to let off a bit of the steam, thereby avoiding an explosion but keeping the basic pressure against the influence of feminine values on public policy, such masculinization stands in the way of humanizing the social order. For, as many feminists would assert, the authentic humanization of society requires a more balanced application of masculine and feminine values. The positive, authentic attributes of each should complement the other and supplant with mutuality and equity the present condition, which distorts these attributes into masculine dominance and feminine submission.

The concept of feminism that informs this monograph does not attribute an innate capacity for greater sensitivity or more moral behavior to women, nor does it assume feminine values and characteristics to be more human or humane than the masculine. Feminism, as it is used here, is one component of a wider humanism conceived as opposition to oppression. It is a belief system that opposes all forms and manifestations of sexism, seeks to abolish them, and assumes that such abolition requires the full and equitable integration of women into all spheres of human activity. Collaterally, it includes the belief that such integration is also necessary to abolish the war system. This is the avowed goal of world order studies.

World Order Values:
Indicators of Militarism and Sexism

World order studies inquire into the possibilities for abolishing war and developing a peaceful and human global order. This inquiry offers the greatest potential for the integration of feminism and feminist perspectives into both peace research and the political struggle for peace. The concept of world order studies, which constitutes the fourth perspective of this work, provides a normative approach to global problems. It projects and evaluates alternatives to the present system that could achieve world order values and open possibilities for the evolution of a more peaceful and just social order. Those who adopt a world order perspective view such evolution as progress toward the universal enjoyment of values that they see as fundamental criteria for the assessment of peace and justice and that they assert should be the basic norms upheld by the structures of a transformed global system. As I will explicate in a later section, these values are somewhat wanting from a feminist perspective in minimal standards for humane norms and global transformation. They do, however, provide us with some basic guidelines for assessing the degree of those antitheses of peace and justice, *violence* (that is, the unnecessary and avoidable harm to life and well-being) and *oppression* (the humanly devised barriers to the exercise of choice and self-determination), which characterize and bind together sexism and the war system. A brief review of world order values is offered here to illustrate this point and to support the case that substantive progress toward either peace or justice cannot be achieved without the elimination of sexism.

Each of the five world order values — economic equity, social justice, ecological balance, political participation, and peace — can be used to demonstrate that the present global order, the war system, is maintained by violence and oppression, and that women are more victimized by the system than are men (Reardon, 1977b). The current severe frustration of these values also suggests the possibility that both increased militarization and the male-chauvinist backlash are symptoms of an authoritarian system responding to a threat to its continuation.

The degree to which economic equity is frustrated by the war machine has been clearly documented each year by *World Military and Social Expenditures*, edited annually by Ruth Sivard. The 1983 report provides data that demonstrate that global poverty is greatly exacerbated as a result of military spending. It also documents an alarming increase in militarization, which is revealed by the number of governments that have fallen under military control, thereby verifying the assertion that public expenditures are an indicator of militarism.

The frustration of the value of economic equity is inevitable in the war system (Melman, 1974). War is by its very nature wasteful. Fornari (1974) points out the relevance of this wastefulness to the psychological roots of war and to the Cold War and the arms race. He provides insights into the psychic causes of the "permanent war economy" and the function of intimidation in the war system.

> The role of the economic motivations of war . . . would appear to be that of rationalizing and obscuring its destructive functions which would, ultimately, also seem to be traceable (on the basis of Bouthoul's investigation of the economic aspects of war as a feast of solemn dissipation and destruction, potlach, etc.) to the sadomasochistic universe of man (Glover, Garma). (pp. 20–21)

> Cold war has all the characteristics of *potlach* or the competitive donation (Marcel Mauss and Georges Bataille). Potlach is an ostentatious gift of considerable value, offered by a tribal chief to his rival. The purpose of the competitive gift is to humiliate, challenge, and obligate the recipient, who in turn must erase the humiliation, accept the challenge, and fulfill the obligation by accepting the gift; later he must retaliate with a more generous and valuable potlach. He must, in other words, return the gift with interest.
>
> Potlach is not only a gift, however. In its most impressive form potlach consists in the solemn *destruction of wealth* [italics added]. A tribal chief presents himself before his rival and has a number of slaves slaughtered before the rival's eyes. The rival must retaliate by slaughtering an even greater number of slaves. Potlach, then, is an act of ostentatious destruction the aim of which is *to intimidate the rival* [italics added] and, ultimately, to give prestige to the donor or destroyer. The present frantic armaments race seems to be a cycle of prodigality-challenge in which each of the adversaries, by wasting an enormous amount of wealth on armaments, hopes to intimidate the other and prove his own superiority. (pp. 18–19)

If we acknowledge that public expenditures also indicate concern for the interests and welfare of women, the United States is an example of the parallel development of militarism and sexism. The recent so-called budget cuts, which have reallocated funds from economic and social programs to the military, have had their most negative effects on women. (Dependent children, minorities, and the aged also have been badly hit; females account for at least half of these.) The number of poverty-line households headed by women has increased dramatically in recent years. Economic disparities, epitomized by the 59 cents versus a dollar wage differential and the 8- versus 16-hour work day comparison between women and men, have long been the most clear and universal indicators of discrimination against women, and are widely documented (ILO, n.d.).

If we define social justice as equity in access to whatever benefits a given society has to offer, it can be observed that militarization not only limits these benefits and makes them less accessible to the poor, it also skews the distribution of benefits to favor the military and those involved in military preparedness and production (for example, cost overruns in military production). Militarization also leads to the classification of certain resources with multiple (military and nonmilitary) uses as strategic, giving military industries priority access to these resources and increasing the valence accorded to military options in policy making (for example, petroleum allocations and strategic metals). Other examples are the offering of advanced education through the military to those who otherwise could not afford it, that is, those with limited access to social benefits; greater availability of research funds to scientists working on defense-related matters; and most especially in the class structure of the military. Although few officers and even fewer in command are of humble origins, it must be admitted that poor boys can make good by succeeding in the military.

Although virtually all human activities require discrimination among alternative possibilities, *negative discrimination* (Reardon, 1977a) — discrimination in access to social benefits on the basis of innate characteristics or other circumstances over which people have no individual control — is, by world order and most other standards of social science, a prime indicator of social injustice. The militarist/sexist norms of the war system are clearly evident in the forms of negative discrimination that characterize the war system. Viewed through feminist and world order lenses the standard discriminatory patterns reveal the most favored groups to be those who appear to offer the most utility to the war-making capacity or are deemed uniquely capable of rendering essential services to it. It is this latter category that accords more

privileges to the scientific and technological elites, privileges formerly reserved to the strategic and command elites. In so doing it has
perverted much scientific endeavor to the purposes of the war system.
Paradoxically, the shift of warfare from an art to a science is responsible for some minor inroads into the traditional discriminatory patterns, which relied more on capacity to plan, command, and guide
in combat than on technological or scientific competence.

If we accept the notion that the social system is primarily a war
system, combat utility can be seen as a fundamental criterion for the
social value placed on human groups. The same phenomenon that
made officer material of those who came to the colors on horseback
and cannon fodder of the foot soldiers may well account for the fact
that men from minority groups often gain access to benefits and
privileges in the military, in industry, and in the professions more easily than women from dominant ethnic groups. (There are exceptions
to this in societies with more complex caste and class structures, notably
Anglo-Indian women and Latin American women. Even when women
of these groups are professionally successful, however, they are still
subject to subtle but very emotionally costly psychosocial discrimination.) Traditionally women had a separate function to serve in the war
system, one which also served industrial economies. Just as a social
analysis from a primarily economic perspective can account for slavery,
racism, and sexism as means of providing cheap labor, and assuring
reproduction of the labor force (the primary function attributed to
women by some such analyses), so a feminist world order analysis can
account for them as deriving from the need to produce and reproduce
cannon fodder. It also could explain why superficial (or regulatory)
rejection of racism and sexism in the armed forces developed more
or less simultaneously with the shift from field combat to technological
warfare and the strategic emphasis on nuclear rather than conventional
weaponry. Population growth has ceased to be a strategic advantage,
and technological warfare does not require cannon fodder.

The tightly and deeply rooted relationship between militarism and
sexism is, I believe, revealed as well in discrimination against the hand-
icapped and homosexuals. The latter case constitutes an especially
malicious form of gynophobia. (As I will note, indoctrination in misogyny is an essential part of basic training.) It should be observed
that occasional homosexual behavior, particularly in all-male environments, is not only tolerated, it carries little social stigma in such environments as prisons and boarding schools. Expulsion from the former
never, and from the latter rarely, occurs as the result of it. Not so with
the military, and certainly not for moral reasons or conventional con-

servatism. Fear of feminine characteristics is essential to military socialization, and with good reason. Homosexual relationships, like heterosexual relationships, run the risk of nurturing a profoundly feminine trait, that of caring as much or more for a loved one as for yourself, frequently taking risks and making sacrifices for his welfare. While as I have observed elsewhere (Reardon, 1981) this is the stuff heroes are made of, it is no way to run an army. As a matter of fact, it is no way to run any institution that depends upon obedience. If men in combat are too concerned for the welfare of a "tender comrade," not only are they likely to be distracted from the task, they will probably be altogether less fierce.

This is not an argument supporting military discrimination against homosexuals, nor do I mean to suggest that homosexual men have any less capacity than women to perform traditional and modern male functions. Neither does it ignore the care and human compassion heterosexual men have shown for comrades in arms. Rather, it is to illuminate what I believe to be a major source of sexist repression, not only in the military but in all authoritarian society: the profound fear of the human capacity to care (Rivers, 1982). It is probably because caring and concern are a threat to unquestioning acceptance of authority that they have been confined primarily to the private and feminine spheres, and why social justice, but not necessarily economic equity, has a low priority in authoritarian societies generally and militarist societies particularly.

Care and concern tend to be person- and relationship-oriented rather than structures- and rules-oriented. When the structures or rules are seen as harmful to persons, particularly related persons (friends, family, dependents), a feminine perspective would bend the rules or go around the structures (Gilligan, 1982). Unquestioning adherence to rules and structures is essential to authoritarianism. Social justice depends more on respect for persons and is less abstract than justice unqualified because it can be conceived and described in personal terms of concrete human experience. Authoritarianism generally ignores social justice issues in these human terms. Frequently, however, especially in socialistically oriented authoritarian governments the social justice issues are translated into economic, structural issues. So, while women and minorities still may be subject to other forms of oppression, they are less likely to be desperately poor. The economic benefits are, however, conceived and distributed in abstract categories, usually defined according to economic function (that is, factory worker, teacher, dependent children). Clever authoritarian states sometimes even can present the image of caring. This is more easily accomplished if the authority is a woman or has a "devoted wife and helpmate." There are more recent cases, but Eva Peron is still a shining example of that class.

Care and concern are also intrinsic to the value of ecological balance. In some ways this value reflects the true genius of the world order approach, for more than any of the others it is truly comprehensive in the sense of functional systems as well as global systems. It is, as well, a life-affirming, relational value that can be pursued only in the context of a reverence for nature. All these attributes make it possible to view ecological balance as the only feminine value of the five that guide world order studies.

Feminine values tend to be more personal and less abstract than masculine values. This is more evident in individual, human indicators than in the institutional ones that masculine values call forth. Although it may seem a contradiction, feminine values are more physical in the bodily sense than are masculine values. This is doubtless because of the mind-body dichotomy that has been fostered mainly by Western culture, an aspect of the same dualism that separates male from female according to masculine and feminine gender attributes. This split attributes mind to the masculine half of the range of human traits and body to the feminine. God may be masculine, the ultimate creator, but the life force and source of nurture is feminine — Mother Nature. (This primal female parent was deified independently, and sometimes in hierarchical superiority, as well as conjointly with male gods by earlier human cultures.) The capacity to give birth, the most fundamental of all biological functions, has been the major identifying characteristic of women. It also has been the factor that has produced the "biology as destiny" syndrome, which has closed women out of intellectual and decision-making functions and left them virtually powerless, "female eunuchs" (Greer, 1971). But it has granted them a special relationship with nature and other mysteries accounting for feminine intuition, that particular form of holistic thinking now recognized as an authentic thought process.

The threat to ecological balance, more than the other world order issues, demonstrates the destructive consequences of the dichotomy between "man" and nature, through which the human species has been led to wage literal war against the natural environment. Also shown is the degree to which the war system itself has been sustained through the matricide of Mother Earth, in the exhaustion of resources and the pollution of the atmosphere resulting from the production and testing of weapons. Ecological destruction is, at its base, misogynist. It is not, as some feminists claim, an example of the notion that masculine forces are death-courting and feminine, life-giving. Rather, it is simply another result of the masculine drive to control and dominate the feminine — a drive, at work in most men and in some women, that is projected by male rule into the larger society. The rape of the Earth is a most apt metaphor for this defilement, a process that has led to the capacity to bring about the death of the ravaged planet. The fate of the Earth would thus parallel the fate of those millions of rape victims who have been murdered as a culmination of the initial crime.

Assessment of the value of political participation reveals sufficient repression in the world political structures to uphold the assertion that the present world order is authoritarian and growing more so through the process of militarization, which is the inevitable consequence of the national security state (Crahan, 1982). The links between militarization and political repression are a central concern of peace research and world order studies, sufficiently documented and widely discussed enough to preclude the necessity of anything more than the briefest mention here.

The two most relevant points to be noted are (1) the psychological factors that incline most of us to accept limitations on participation when the national security is said to be threatened, and (2) the relationship of women's participation to the level of political freedom and democratic participation in general. As mentioned earlier, the more repressive a regime is, the more sexist it is likely to be. Sexism, militarism, and repression are emotionally conditioned, produced by fear, strengthened by intimidation, and maintained largely as a consequence of the paralysis of the critical capacities of the citizenry. As Fornari (1974) observes:

> In dealing with the problem of the emotional implications of the phenomenon of war, Bouthoul reaches the conclusion that it is sufficient to convince people that they are threatened in order to induce them to give up their rights. He consequently defines sovereignty as *"the right granted to one to intimidate others."* (p. 27)

> One of the most typical effects of the warlike impulse is that it dulls the critical sense of the people, paralyzing above all their ability to evaluate the destruction rationally. (p. 31)

The second point brought to light by sexism in politics is an indication that most of our present political structures and practices are rooted in patriarchy. Contrary to von Clausewitz, politics as the exercise of power is more an outgrowth of the war system than the other way around, for politics as much as war is an essentially masculine enterprise. This is an assertion that stems from the fact that politics is, even today, primarily conducted by men, according to masculine standards, and in the masculine style. Success in politics as in warfare is viewed as evidence of masculinity and requires its own degree of ferocity (Brock-Utne, 1981, pp. 33–37, 50–51). Nothing attests to this requirement more than the political performances of the world's most powerful women, who have to continue proving their toughness even (especially) after they have reached the heights of power.

Women's exclusion from political power, which persists generations after the granting of the franchise in most Western countries, is a significant factor in maintaining the war system. This is a factor becoming acutely evident as women become more politicized in their peace efforts, and as the differences between male and female voters on security issues become more pronounced, causing the media to report frequently on the gender gap.

The feminist political scientist Judith Stiehm, starting from the Weberian "definition of the state as the institution holding a monopoly on the legitimate use of force within a specified geographic area," provides us with another insight into the sexism/war system connection garnered from the concept of political participation.

Basically the argument is that the state's defining function is that of managing society's force. Yet, women are everywhere forbidden access to the use of state force. The result is that they are everywhere less than citizens no matter what the law says and no matter what their self-perception. . . . Some effort has also been made to explain women's absence from elected and appointed offices. Some authors, of course, give "nature" as an explanation; others point to careers interrupted by child-bearing, to women's lack of legal training and/ or to male prejudice. If we go back to Weber, however, another possibility emerges. That is that the basic and monopoly function of the state is to exercise force for, with, and on its citizens. If women will not, cannot, or, if it is thought that they will not or cannot exercise force, they are poor candidates for offices with coercive responsibility. Indeed, the public seems to find women most acceptable as government officials when they serve as judges; they are also acceptable in legislative bodies where they may help to provide a budget for and make rules about the coercive forces (the police and the military); and they seem to be least acceptable as executives, as the officials who must implement by personally giving direction. This is not necessarily an irrational view for only a limited number

of women obtain any training, either theoretical or practical, in ex-
ecutive duties. (Stiehm, 1979)

There is some reason to suspect, too, that women are kept out of
disarmament talks because the objective of such talks is clearly not
disarmament (Johansen, 1978a). Feminists observing the Second U.N.
Special Session on Disarmament (SSDII) expressed, virtually from
the first day, doubts about any positive outcomes. There were even
fewer women delegates than at SSDI, where there were only a handful.

There is, of course, for very good reason, fear of women's equal
participation in politics. While the antifeminist women may fear that
full citizenship will mean military service, there is an even deeper fear
among the male power structure of what political equality may mean
for the entire system. Most of all, if women enter politics and share
equitably in power, the essence of maleness, then what will happen
to the masculine identity so dependent on the one-upmanship of not
being a woman? Jewish feminists note the consciousness-raising effect of traditional prayers in which men thank God for not having been
born a woman. Excluding women from politics and war is a primary
means of preventing them from regaining the total control remembered
from men's childhoods and of maintaining masculine identity, an identity derived in part in separation from their mothers and thus from
all women. Fear of losing that identity runs even deeper than the fear
referred to by Caryl Rivers (1982) in "ERA's Death and the Fear of
New Women," in which she states that all women will become like
men if they achieve political equality. (As Rivers points out, this is
also a fear of losing the free lunch based on women's unpaid labor.)

Peace as a world order value generally connotes what peace research defines as negative peace, the absence of war. So defined, the
major force operating against the value is the arms race. No other factor manifests more completely the links between sexism and militarism
than does the arms race, particularly the nuclear arms race. Nor does
any other factor reveal more precisely the sexism, in Garcia Chafardet's
sense of the distortion of maleness and femaleness so as to maintain
female inferiority, that lies at the core of the war system. The distortion of sexuality into masculine and feminine roles and behavior accounts for one of the most fundamental impediments to peace: fear.
Security concerns, economic preoccupations, ideological intransigence,
even death denial are secondary to the basic and fundamental fear that
is the real obstacle to disarmament: castration anxiety (Fornari, 1974).

The phallicism of weaponry in general and the nuclear arms race
in particular has been noted by feminists and a few psychiatrists (For-

nari, 1974, p. 98), but little attended to by policy makers or researchers grappling with obstacles to disarmament. Yet it is the most manifest
psychological factor at play in all the machismo of the arms race and
in the approach/avoidance behaviors evident in arms control and disarmament negotiations. It also helps to explain why some women pursue disarmament more vigorously than men, and reveals a potentially
crucial and significant link between male identity and war. If women
can become like men by engaging in politics, men may become like
women if they cannot make war anymore. And, as every female is
imbued with a terror of the "fate worse than death" that is the "dishonor"
of rape, so every male is taught from childhood to fear the possibility
of being like a woman. Such fates (being an effeminate man or a
dishonored woman) are shunned in ways analogous to the "better dead
than Red" and "death before dishonor" mentality that supports militarism. And, I sincerely believe, this mentality has profoundly influenced the events that have brought us to the life-and-death crisis of
the nuclear arms race.

Most readers of scandalous popular books expected only titilla-
tion from a recent bestseller celebrating the joyous sexual liberation
of contemporary America as the emergence of a phallic culture. The
description of the Kennedy administration as the phallic presidency
seemed no more than a sensational exposé of the participation of the
best and brightest in that liberation movement (Talese, 1980). However, those revelations actually gave new insights into the "missile gap"
issue of the presidential campaign, some rather chilling ones about
the machismo of American foreign policy and our phallic approach
to national security. The allusion also foreshadowed the notion of
nuclearism put forth by Robert Lifton (Lifton & Falk, 1982), the observation that we have virtually come to worship the weapons. We are
reminded of the phallus worship of very early warriors, and, I would
hope, are called to pay greater attention to the profound, intertwined
psychological roots of sexism and the war system. Without a greater
comprehension of how these roots affect our political behavior and our
political institutions, peace, the first and fundamental world order
value, stands little chance of fulfillment.

World order values, I believe, are a humane and universal set of
values that could serve as criteria for the vision of a preferred global
order. They provide guidelines for the derivation of new institutions
designed to assure a peaceful and just social order. The pursuit of these
social values lies in the realm of institution building, mainly politics.
However, the generation of the political force and the mobilization
of people in support of these values necessitates concern and commit-

ment of a nature that is profoundly personal. Each of us needs to understand in both the structural, explicit sense of society and politics and the subtle, implicit sense of the human mind how thoroughly we have been conditioned to the war system and its sexist foundations. Our very selves and the historic condition in which we find ourselves have evolved from the intricate and intimate interplay between the psychological forces and the sociopolitical structures that give rise to our culture. Sexism and war are cultural problems that cannot be illuminated, much less resolved, by either an exclusively psychological or a solely structural approach, any more than they can be resolved in isolation from each other. The notion of *reciprocal causation* seems to me to offer the possibility of providing both the knowledge and the strategies that appropriately and effectively combine the personal and the political into a single strategy for overcoming the twin problems of sexism and war.

Chapter 3

ENEMIES AND VICTIMS: THE MILITARIST-SEXIST SYMBIOSIS

SOME FEMINISTS are now asking the question, Is peace possible in a patriarchal society? If we define peace as a condition in which world order values prevail for the majority of the Earth's people, the answer clearly is no! Peace and patriarchy are antithetical by definition.

> Patriarchy is the rule of the fathers. It is a system of male headship, male domination, male power — a system of controlling women through economic dependence, violence, and domestication — a system which assigns women to the private sphere of home and family and directs white males to the public sphere of work and decision-making.
>
> Patriarchy is a system of dualisms: mind over body, thinking over feeling, heaven over earth, spirit over flesh — dualisms in which women are identified with the negative side. Patriarchy is a system of values developed through male experience: competition, hierarchy, aggression, bureaucracy, alienation from the earth, denial of emotion, generational shortsightedness, the objectification of other, whether it be of sex, race, or class. (Zanotti, 1979)

This dualism is also manifest in war, a competitive game requiring aggressors and victims who play through the deadly combative ritual to achieve status and be recognized as winners or losers. Most often the aggressor becomes the winner. Aggressors also need enemies. The role of enemy is the common denominator. In the war system everyone is and has an enemy, and all are either winners or losers. As societies we strive for the winner role, but as persons defined by sex, men are conditioned to play winners and women losers. (In this aspect racism is also a significant component of the game, with whites the winners and people of color the losers.) These are their fundamental roles in patriarchy. Although patriarchy certainly has not precluded loving, caring, generous fathers, it has tended to impede the development of those particular human attributes in men. Men are socialized for authority and responsibility rather than for care and love; women are socialized for submission and dependence rather than for assertion and autonomy.

Patriarchy has also legitimated the use of force to assist those in authority to impose their wills on those subject to them. Granted, this imposition is based on the assumption that the will of the authority is in the best interest of all concerned because it stems from superior knowledge and wisdom. As subjects, both men and women are expected to accept the forceful imposition of the will of the authority, but men are expected to develop the capacity to impose their own will on others lower in the authority chain, whereas women have been trained not only to accept imposition but to accommodate totally to it. They must be as pleasing as possible to authority figures, never anger them or risk more forceful, even violent, imposition. Much so-called feminine behavior, accommodation and wiles, is the consequence of this particular condition, which requires mechanisms for coping with authoritarianism and avoiding violence. Men are conditioned to be aggressive and ready to use violence and women are conditioned to fear and avoid it.

Threat as System Maintenance: The Issue of Rape

In patriarchal society persons are bred to violence and authoritarianism: to cope with it and to impose it. It is developed in us from our earliest days. Indeed, some see patriarchy itself as the fundamental cause of war and oppression (Mallmann, 1978).

The authority structures that pervade the military also pervade the entire society. The fundamental willingness to use violence against others on which warfare depends is conditioned by early training and continuous socialization in patriarchal society. All are taught to respect authority, that is, fear violence. Men are conditioned to deal with their fear of violence by developing the capacity to use it competitively with "equals" and oppressively on "inferiors." Women are conditioned to deal with the fear of violence, not only by developing behaviors of accommodation and avoidance but also by learning to cope with it as a fundamental given of the human condition. Because they must cope with and avoid violence, women are permitted to express their fear of it. Demonstration of fear is feminine in women but cowardly in men. The sexist conspiracy, however, secretly communicates to boys that, although macho men do know fear, they simply do not show it. Indeed, boys and men are encouraged to become more fierce, more aggressive when they feel fear. Fear in men is channeled into aggression, in women into submission, for such behaviors are necessary to maintain patriarchal authoritarianism. Aggression and submission are also the core of the basic relations between men and women, accounting, many believe, for women's toleration of male chauvinism. Some assert that these behaviors are the primary cause of all forceful exploitation, and account for perhaps the most significant common characteristic of sexism and the war system: rape.

Rape essentially is forcing a person or persons into submission and accommodation by the threat or use of force and violence. There are analogies to sexual assault in the treatment of enemies and subject peoples that indicate that submission to force in order to survive makes both sexism and the war system possible. Were it not for the possibility that wars could be won and that women would continue to accept sexist domination, neither system could be perpetuated. Both assume that at base most human beings hold *physical* survival as the highest value.

"From prehistoric times to the present, I believe rape has played a critical function. It is nothing more or less than a conscious process of intimidation by which all men keep all women in a state of fear" (Brownmiller, 1976). Rape, as the term is used here by Brownmiller, is to male-female relations what the behavior of conquering troops is to occupied territories, what the trappings of imperial authority are to colonialism. Rape in various forms has been a traditional war system device used for symbolic or deterrent purposes as well as the basic intimidating mechanism to maintain submission. A secretary of state who talks about a demonstration use of a nuclear weapon displays the same underlying motives as the right-wing terrorists who rape and murder women missionaries working for people the right-wingers see as involved in a left-wing or communist struggle. The system, however, obscures the evidence that "nuke rattling" and politically motivated sexual assault are aspects of the same phenomenon. This is demonstrated by the virtual failure of most media to report that the American churchwomen murdered in El Salvador in December 1980 were also raped. In an article in the *National Catholic Reporter* it was noted, "A special message was sent to us by the rapists and murderers of the four American women. They wanted to make it clear that women who step out of their place will find no special protection behind the labels of 'nun or churchworker.' Or even 'American'" (Papa, 1981).

Rape is, indeed, a deliberate device to keep women in line. Although Mary Bader Papa, author of the *National Catholic Reporter* article, does not quote Brownmiller, her insight coincides with that expounded in *Against Our Will*. It also clearly demonstrates that rape is, as Brownmiller asserts, a conscious tactic of warfare. Rape, as asserted in this monograph, is the ultimate metaphor for the war system, wherein violence is the final arbiter of social relations and force is the mortar holding together the structure of the public order.

The continuation of warfare depends primarily on the readiness of the parties involved to use violence against one another. Without it the fundamental threat system that maintains the basic relationship both between men and women and among competing nation-states could not function. Such readiness appears to derive from two sources: first, permission, or social and/or political legitimation to carry out violent and aggressive impulses, and second, dehumanization of the other in the relationship. The reinforcement of otherness, coupled with rationalizing the lesser worthiness of the other, facilitates the alienation that can push competitive but inequitable relationships into violent conflict. Sexist alienation of male from female results from the rejection — even to the point of despisement to assure that rejection — of "feminine" characteristics in boys and men and "masculine" characteristics in women. Sexist alienation is, I believe, a fundamental basis for alienation in general and negative otherness perceptions in particular. The development of enemy images, indeed, might not be possible were not all human beings socialized into negative otherness from birth.

Otherness connotes not only human differences but also, in its negative form, hierarchies in human worth, the fundamental assumption that makes possible the dehumanization of the other sex, another race or class, citizens of another state, or adherents to another political philosophy. Clearly, some forms of otherness are required for human survival. Distinguishing between male and female is a biological necessity for the reproduction of the species. Separation from the nurturing parent is necessary for the normal development of the person. Cultural differences are required for successful human adaptation to various environments. Distinction, separation, and difference are natural devices for maintaining a multiplicity of life forms on a complex, living planet. What is at question are the uses beyond biological necessity to which human society has put otherness. Sexism and the war system are both violent uses. In essence, violence is unnecessary harm, a definition that assumes that alternative means to achieve the same goal have been ignored or rejected. Although it may be argued that in the past both warfare and male chauvinism were employed for survival purposes, this argument is not totally convincing. Without doubt both raise more threats to than defenses for human survival (Divale & Harris, 1976).

The permission society accords men to maintain dominion over women by the threat and use of violence can be viewed as a significant cause of most forms of violence, both overt and structural. It is a kind of license, derived from glands, to control and dominate. Because violence, as here defined, is unnecessary harm, it is therefore a consequence of choice. Our society chooses to use violence. A society that deems wife beating to be a private matter between spouses, not subject to civil interference, is not likely to admit that excessive exploitation of female labor is a significant problem of economic equity. The same tacit approval that perpetuates rape seems to operate in New York sweatshops and Third World factories.

The extent of this permission and the degree to which violence operates in the relations between men and women are becoming more apparent. Feminist research is beginning to reveal how many experiences formerly deemed seduction were in fact consummated through various forms of intimidation, if not force, and to expose how many women have been attacked by men with whom they are acquainted. This license to use force is also reinforced by the blaming-the-victim syndrome, which insists that the victim provoked the attack — much as the aggression of one state against another has been rationalized by the aggressor as the consequence of provocation. Social scientists and lawyers have had equally difficult and, I would submit, similar problems in defining both rape and armed aggression. The connection between these acts, however, has seldom been noted, and then mainly by feminists whose central, sometimes only, concern is the former.

Considering frustration as a cause of violence and aggression also brings forth some interesting parallels between sexism and the war system and the need for enemies and victims. Arbitrary limitations on human behavior produce resentment and anger. The more severe the limitations, the more explosive is the potential for violent reaction, and the greater is the psychological need for an enemy. Indeed, it is probable that much of the hopeless counterviolence of the oppressed and exploited is the inevitable consequence of frustrated development potential, as well as righteous anger. Society even permits a certain amount of such counterviolence, rather than change the basic threat/force system. In fact, this kind of violence helps to justify the need for a vigilant and often oppressive police apparatus, another arm of the patriarchal system. Sometimes it even sanctions certain forms of counterviolence by foregoing punishment or providing minimal fulfillment of the frustrated desires. So it is that women who have murdered their attackers are sometimes let off by enlightened juries, and violent civil disturbances can produce some token social programs. These are meager concessions for keeping the system intact.

When we consider the degree to which the socialization of boys imposes more severe frustration than that of girls, the greater aggressiveness in men and boys than in women and girls seems inevitable. Not only are they subject to more pressures to reject the human attributes associated with the other sex, but their roles and behavioral repertoires are less flexible and more subject to social scrutiny. The social expectations of the male role are more rigid and demanding of performance. It has been observed that parents and teachers are more permissive with boys than with girls, but the nature of what is permitted must also be acknowledged. Boys are permitted to be more unruly (that is, physically expressive) and adventurous, and to manipulate the environment so long as they do not tamper with the general order. In some ways this permissiveness can be looked on as comparable to chivalry. It is a compensatory advantage awarded for bearing the greater social expectations. Such permissiveness is also an opportunity for boys to learn their social roles as aggressors, intimidators, and protectors against "enemies." In a convergence of negative interest, boys even learn to collaborate with "enemies" to perpetuate the system. (Certain competitive team sports are practice for such collaboration.) Men are socialized to be warriors, in the roles of either enemies or aggressors, while women are socialized to be victims and surrogate enemies. Each sex is trained to its role, not born to it. Although sexism and the war system are deeply rooted in the human psyche, neither is instinctual or innate (any more than slavery is natural, or that any particular human future is inevitable, that is, insusceptible to value choice). Both, like all social behavior, are learned, and both are subject to change through learning. Indeed, the attribution of sex role separation (as well as sexism, human aggression, and war) to human nature is a perversion of science, for it functions as a rationalization for refusing to pursue knowledge of alternatives.

Barbara Stanford, a peace researcher whose work is directed toward developing the requisite learning goals and processes for the achievement of peace (one of the few who has devoted research efforts to both sexism and war), has undertaken a broad study of theories of aggression. Her study, like my own speculations on the links between sexism and the war system, was initially motivated by concern with overcoming obstacles to disarmament. Her research has revealed parallel insights about aggressive behavior.

Aggression, at least in healthy individuals, does not arise spontaneously, but as a response to specific stimuli, although the number of stimuli that may be responded to aggressively may be quite varied and the threshold for response may be quite low.

According to Fromm, "the conclusion seems unavoidable that aggressive behavior of animals is a response to any kind of threat to survival, or as I would prefer to say more generally to the vital interests of the animal whether as an individual or as a member of its species" (Fromm, 1973, p. 95). Research on the physiology of aggression by Mark and Ervin demonstrates that there is no physiological mechanism for spontaneous buildup of aggressive impulses. Johnson (1972) also researched the conclusion that aggression is a response to stimuli not a spontaneous drive.

Aggression, then, is one possible behavior resulting from a state of physiological arousal which is a response to a threat of some kind. The state of physiological arousal is very common because the stimuli are quite frequent. Sterns (1972, p. 55) notes that the anger response has a "100% incidence rate." Anger, hostility and other states of arousal associated with aggression, however, do not have to lead to aggression. They may cause the person to flee or the person may ignore the feelings or act in any number of other ways. Not all aggressive behavior, of course, is associated with feelings of anger or hostility. Some is coldly rational, but rational behavior is by definition not a spontaneous instinct. So, while current research demonstrates that aggressive feelings are universal among normal humans, aggression is not a spontaneous drive. (Stanford, 1981)

Stanford's research indicates that aggression is largely a matter of conscious choice and complements the thesis that rigid sex role and sexual identity separation is a significant factor contributing to socially sanctioned violence. It also suggests that the provocations most likely to lead to selecting force and violence from the entire repertoire of possible behaviors are those perceived as threats to vital interests, the very behaviors reinforced by sexism and the war system. It is the belief of many feminists that society at large sees male superiority as a vital interest, just as nation-states view war-making capacity as a vital interest. Both require legitimating the use of violence by male authority structures.

We might also note that the level of violence seen as necessary relates to the severity of the perceived threat. This phenomenon has been observed in many repressive systems under attack. For example, authoritarian regimes become more repressive, use torture more, and tend to crack down on dissidents when the level of dissidence and resistance rises. Similarly, the more threatened the male power structure feels as a result of women's liberation efforts, the more violent will be the treatment of women. The increase in the number of violent attacks on women, in wife beating, and in the depiction of such events in films and the arts (e.g., social acceptance of pornography involving explicit violence against women) is viewed by many, not only feminists, as a reaction to the women's liberation movement — a male chauvinist backlash (Siskel, 1981–82).

Evidence that this hypothesis is worthy of exploration can be found in a review of the history of the women's movement, at least in modern Europe and the United States. There is a possible relationship between the increased agitation for removing restrictions that classified women as property and prevented them from exercising economic rights, the struggle for suffrage and for full equality, and the development of more powerful weaponry for use against larger numbers of noncombatant and nonmilitary targets.

I do not believe that it is a mere coincidence that these radical changes, the potential total transformation implied by the full equality of women to men, emerge simultaneously with the potential of modern weaponry to totally destroy human society as we know it. The humanizing transformation implied by the complete equality of women and men is of equal dimension to the dehumanizing destruction of nuclear war. Is women's demand for authentic equality perhaps the ultimate provocation calling forth the ultimate threat?

Another parallel phenomenon worthy of study is the masculinization of the technology that made weapons development possible. The sexually designated functions of traditional societies were performed with an appropriate technology. Both men and women had access to particular (sometimes different but complementary) technological know-how, which not only made it possible for them to perform their respective functions but also provided sign and symbol of the social value of those functions. The modern technology of Western industrial society has excluded women from technical knowledge and from the scientific research from which it was derived. Women's function in industrial technology became as objectified as women themselves had become in male-dominated society. As cheap factory labor they constituted nothing more than an extension of the productive machines. Their bodies reproduced the labor force and in the patriarchal mode this meant that children, too, were used as virtual machine parts. It cannot go unobserved that children as well as women were and still are sorely victimized by patriarchy. This is well demonstrated by the contemporary plague of multifarious forms of child abuse. Nor can it be overlooked that this industrial development accompanied the imperial expansion of Europe and its domination of what is today called the Third World (Sakamoto, 1981).

Even more to the point, the masculinization of technology made it virtually inevitable that technology would be guided by masculine perceptions and values into the development of tools for coercion and imposition at the expense of care and needs fulfillment. The process may have made the ultimate weapons inevitable. Possession of these weapons has become as important an indication of power and prestige to nation-states as the ability to exert physical force is to the masculine identity of men in the patriarchal structures in which we live. Men's education and socialization prepares them to manifest this identity as warriors, the wielders of weapons. I assert that exploration of these socialization patterns is vitally significant to uncover the insights and knowledge necessary to avoid the destruction of civilization, and to reverse the trend toward the development of more and more "sophisticated" weapons of mass destruction, which drains off so many of the resources required to meet the just demands of women and all the world's oppressed peoples.

Weapons are both a significant factor in masculine identity and a crucial factor in the functioning of patriarchy. Although weaponry is not so absolutely essential in maintaining the oppression of women as it is in keeping other oppressed groups in line, it serves one of the most vital functions of the war system. It produces victims. Whereas enemies, though despised as the embodiment of all the negative characteristics we see in ourselves, are at least equals, victims never are. They are innocent of the sins we project onto our enemies, and they are weaker. Innocence and vulnerability are two of the most cherished and admired feminine characteristics. Women are socialized to manifest these traits as men are socialized to display the attributes of the warrior. They thus collaborate in their own oppression, as do other oppressed groups, by acting out their assigned characteristics, and in so doing, they provide an impetus to the continued production of weapons (so that they may be protected or avenged).

Patriarchy depends on the vulnerability of women. The war system feeds on it. No wonder more massive weaponry has developed as more women refuse to remain vulnerable and seek to meet the challenges of equality — even when doing so may mean that they become acknowledged, not only implicit, enemies. Indeed, I would argue that this is fundamental to the concept of deterrence. What is to be deterred, even to the point of the ultimate threat from the ultimate weapons, is liberation of the oppressed, the global achievement of human equality, particularly women's equality. Women's equality is so strong a threat to sexist masculine identity that it is perceived as a threat to the very being of man. As the women's struggle became stronger, so too the weapons of war became more destructive and less discriminate. Women, children, and the aged became objects of attack, not only in the pillage and looting that followed the battle, but even in the battle itself. And clearly they are the victims of deterrent weapons produced at the expense of their own social and economic needs. As runaway slaves and "uppity niggers" were subject to the most horrible of retributions, so women in their struggle for full humanity may have provoked the most horrible of retributions for having threatened the "natural order." The Aztecs sacrificed the flower of their civilization's youth to appease their gods and keep the natural order in place; for centuries we have sacrificed ours to the gods of war. Now a scientific and military nuclear priesthood seeks to deter the change in the "natural order" that promises to transcend the social differences between men and women. Their retribution entails not only forcing women back into vulnerability by a threat to their lives, but includes as well a threat to the one power patriarchy could not take from women, that of giving life; this time all life. We have invoked the wrath of the fathers and they have responded, "Our way or no way!"

This "deterrence theory" of patriarchal retribution is admittedly not so readily evident as that which ascribes the arms race to the desire to deter the liberation of the Third World, but it is at base derived from the same set of ever more evident conditions—the desperate and violent behavior of a creature under extreme threat of death. World order studies recognize this connection in such work as that of Jan Oberg (1981), which illuminates the repressive purpose of the arms race and links it incontrovertibly to structural violence. Surely, if only in recognition of the need to understand fully the interrelationships among parallel social phenomena that are integral to world order studies, the field must give some consideration to the possibility of links between the arms race and sexist repression.

Structural Violence: Systematic Oppression Based on Human Differences

Oppression is the most significant manifestation of structural violence. Most frequently it is based on sex, race, and class and, in some cases, on culture, age, or politics. One of the major mechanisms for sustaining oppression is the process of the acculturation of the oppressed, which Frantz Fanon and Paolo Freire, among others, have suggested results in their internalization of the image of the oppressor. This internalization is, I believe, a coping device that enables the oppressed to survive by accepting (or giving the appearance of accepting) the values and world view of the oppressor rather than engaging in a struggle against the oppressor that likely would lead to self-destruction. Thus oppressed peoples frequently have rationalized their condition by accepting the assertion of the oppressor that he is superior and entitled to privilege because he exemplifies an ideal form of humanity. Many oppressed peoples have accepted a sense of their own inferiority as the price of survival.

As Garcia Chafardet points out, this phenomenon not only devalues the intrinsic characteristics of the oppressed, it also adds to the chain of oppression, holds hierarchical relations in place, and continues to produce enemies and victims.

> This prevailing socialization process [i.e., socialization of the oppressed] has conditioned human beings, to a greater or lesser degree, to feel superior or inferior to each individual with whom she or he interrelates. It seems that the more we fear and resent higher authority the more we tend to oppress those we perceive as inferior. (Garcia Chafardet, 1978)

Garcia Chafardet attributes the male-female form of hierarchy to the greater physical strength that men were able to manifest in the earliest stages of human society, thereby according physical strength the capacity to determine inferiority and superiority. If, as asserted by such peace researchers as Johan Galtung (1980), it is true that all unequal relations are essentially conflictual, there has been a battle between the sexes since the earliest days of civilization. It is quite understandable that most human beings believe that war is the consequence of human nature, for our entire history as a species has been characterized by contention and conflict among and between people, starting with the fundamental conflict between men and women (Brownmiller, 1976).

A major coping device by which women have sustained themselves in this conflict of inequality is the "If you can't beat 'em, join 'em" strategy. Women's acceptance of male superiority has been almost as much a contributing factor to sexism as men's exercise of intimidation and force. Thus there is some evidence to uphold the thesis that there can be no oppressive system without the assent of the oppressed.

It seems equally evident that the oppressed do battle in their own way. In a sense, many of the negative "feminine" characteristics are manifestations of the earliest type of guerilla warfare against an oppressor. Deception, obstructionism, recalcitrance, and unwelcome surprises are standard elements in nonformal warfare. What Garcia Chafardet refers to as games of victimization that women engage in also are engaged in by men and are part of the standard behavioral repertoire of the oppressor as well. There is a tacit agreement that the oppressor will complain but not respond with destructive force to these tactics, for there is, after all, no need. These tactics, in fact, keep the system in place, and therefore are to the oppressor's advantage. The oppressor is aware of the battle waged by the oppressed, looks on it with contempt and disdain, but continues to tolerate it. I was, for example, dismayed but not surprised to hear a Catholic priest say, in discussing aspects of the confessional, "Women are totally incapable of telling the truth. I really don't expect that what they say is what has indeed happened."

These attitudes demonstrate not only techniques of oppression but also the painful lack of understanding between men and women. Much of this lack of understanding, this communication gap, is doubtless a result of the psychosocial conditioning that seems to reify anatomical differences. Men are conditioned to develop pragmatic minds that deal with the concrete and quantifiable. The ideal masculine mind is precise, technical, and logical in the sense that masculine thought is expected to follow the scientific mode of observing and analyzing reality. He must *know* the reality, the environment, which he must control. Women are conditioned to be intuitive, sensitive, and feeling, more in touch with the emotions than with reason. They must *sense* their environment in dimensions beyond the empirical. Men are perceived to be rational, women emotional and irrational, and therefore not to be trusted with serious responsibility. Women who have become successful in a man's world are generally those who have demonstrated superior mastery of logic, reason, or the scientific method. They do not overtly exhibit emotion and intuition. Men and women are conditioned to think differently and to speak virtually different languages.

At its worst, this communication gap is manifest in the outrage with which women often hear what men have to say and the distraction if not the disdain with which men often listen to women. It also may account for the modes of violence each tends to impose on the other and to experience from the social system. Whereas physical violence against women is a serious problem for many women, the structural violence of oppression and discrimination affects all women. Structural violence victimizes all men and women in oppressed groups and nations, but relatively few men (even in the most oppressed classes) have been subject to the physical violence of an outraged woman who pursues vengeance by furiously striking out at her innocent man. Structurally oppressed men frequently give vent to their frustration in wife beating and gain a sense of worth by structural dominance over women (Garcia Chafardet, 1975). Most women, accepting that they are physically weaker, resort to henpecking and other forms of harassment, disdain, verbal abuse, and "the silent treatment." When the behavior hits its mark, the women are characterized as castrating or by other more colorful sexist adjectives. For if a man is bested by a woman he is no longer a "real man." If force is not an option for him, his best bet is to ignore the situation or at least to keep his cool, much as the power establishment reacts to the "outbursts" of disarmament demonstrations.

Similar dynamics have occurred in many professional settings, including peace research institutes. Power structures in academia, the family, or the polity tend to avoid controversial communication, particularly messages that are pregnant with possibilities for change. This has been painfully evident in the response to the disarmament movement. In spite of vigorous public dissent and protest, the foreign policy establishment does not hear the message. (As the secretary of defense told one million disarmament demonstrators after June 12, 1982, U.S. foreign policy is not made on the Great Lawn of Central Park.) Neither has shrewish behavior made the slightest dent in the armor of patriarchy. The powerful choose not to hear, for it is essential for the oppressor, too, to maintain sufficient "innocence" to rationalize his position in the structures of society.

Communication also tends to break down enemy images, which are so essential to the perceptual apparatus of the war system. Women constantly complain that men do not listen to them. The complaint is usually stated to indicate that the men are too busy or uncaring or, more often, insensitive. What women do not usually acknowledge is that men must guard against hearing them. They must not know the substance of women's concerns, or understand the human costs of those concerns, for knowledge and understanding might lead to acceptance and change. When men do respond to women's complaints it is often to reject them, usually in anger or derision, or less frequently to admit to some sin or fault that is easily shrugged off and usually never rectified. Some of these same dynamics can be seen in arms negotiations, wherein the point is not to understand the position of the other side, but to come out ahead in the interchange.

The communication gap serves a significant purpose of patriarchy. It is important to keep a manageable degree of hostility alive in the adversary, so that the motor of the system may idle f͏ ͏ ͏ ͏ ͏ to time, but it is never fully switched off. There are devices ͏ior ͏th͏ purpose fashioned from the rejection of the characteristics of the adver͏ sary. For example, there may be no masculine characteristic that infuriates women more than men's insistence on rational discourse regarding emotional issues, whether about personal relationships or the genetic effects of low-level radiation. Perhaps nothing arouses more contempt of feminine modes than the insistence on consideration of the feelings involved in issues and problems. This aspect of the communication gap is an acutely serious one representing a significant obstacle to constructive collaboration between feminism and the peace movement, especially in these times when the issues of survival are explored in such an emotionally charged atmosphere. The work of Carole Gilligan (1982), a Harvard psychologist, illuminates women's modes of moral reasoning and presently constitutes the only evident research holding some promise of narrowing this gap.

The most explicit description, a classic case study so to speak, of the communication gap is to be found in a feminist novel, *The Bleeding Heart* (French, 1981). The dialogues between the two main characters, a man and woman who care for and constantly talk to each other, exemplify it perfectly. For all the talk, neither character comes fully to comprehend the other. They illustrate in a sharply recognizable way the difference of world views between those who uphold the established order characterized by masculine modes emphasizing rationality and those who advocate transformational policy as a shift toward feminine modes emphasizing care. It is no accident that Marilyn French, a feminist writer, attributes the latter world view to the woman of this couple, whose discourse brilliantly denounces contemporary social structures and their impacts on individual, reflective human beings.

This different psychic conditioning also produces some different attitudes toward sexuality and sexual activities that have relevance to the threat system. They reflect another way in which anatomical differences are endowed with significance beyond reproductive function in order to intensify the social differences between the sexes. Women, probably because of their responsibility for the welfare of children, are conditioned to personalize sexuality and place it within the context of close caring relationships, traditionally marriage. Men, on the other hand, traditionally have been conditioned to objectify and depersonalize sex in order to maintain the distance and fissure between the sexes. Most men are thus able to objectify virtually all women, except those for whom society has given them special responsibilities, mainly female relatives. Much as the nation-state encourages citizens to accept violence against those outside the national boundaries but generally prohibits it against those within, men are conditioned to protect and cherish the women for whom they have been given responsibility but to have little or no concern for other women. This psychic conditioning makes women emotionally dependent on men as well as physically vulnerable to them. Even more importantly, it makes it easier for men to objectify whole groups of people, and therefore it becomes less difficult to rationalize the use of violence against them. Thus it is to be expected that women are more likely to show concern for peace and fear of war than men, not because it is inherent in their hormonal systems, but because of their social conditioning to focus on the human and personal.

At base, because men are conditioned to be warriors and women to be wives and mothers, there is a social expectation that warfare will take place on battlegrounds, in board rooms, at professional conventions, in the marketplace, and any locus where men compete. Because men always must be ready to do battle, society gives them tacit permission to practice in more private, even intimate, settings, and conspires through sex-role separation to produce the "intimate enemy," the fundamental relationship that makes possible many subsequent enemy relationships. The relation to the intimate enemy, like the basic misogyny cultivated by total dependence on the mother, serves to instruct men in those feelings toward an enemy that serve as the enabling mechanism for the legal mayhem, rape, and murder which is war. The intimate enemy is found in the closest human relationships — the mother against whom we struggle for individuation, the spouse with whom we contend to maintain individuality, and the presence of the other in ourselves whom we must exorcise to assure our individual identity as a man or a woman. Both sexes struggle with the intimate enemy.

As we have observed that human beings are born into a state of warfare, we also might suggest that the most devastating and painful battles are the consequence of *Combat in the Erogenous Zones* (Bengis, 1972). The battle between the sexes takes place not only in intimate relationships but within each human being. The sense of frustration at having been cut off from a whole range of human characteristics is inevitable, given what I believe to be a Procrustean, limiting socialization into sex role differences. As William Sloane Coffin, senior minister at New York's Riverside Church and member of the board of the World Policy Institute, has said frequently, "The woman most in need of liberation is the woman within every man."

A similar point is made by Nancy Chodorow (1978), who indicates that the individuation process in boys usually involves very strong rejection of the feminine as they separate from their mothers. Both Chodorow and Gilligan (1982) observe this rejection as a crucial element in the developmental process that leads men to emphasize individualism over relationship, accounting for a major and perhaps the most significant difference between men and women. Although the separation process in a girl requires some rejection of the mother and therefore the feminine, it does not require rejection of the other. However, society sees to it that she stifles masculine attributes. If there is some tolerance of androgyny in childhood, it must be put aside with other childish things at puberty, at least stored if not discarded. So it also might be said that there is a masculine persona imprisoned in every woman. What greater oppression can human beings experience than imprisonment or enslavement? What greater violence than the death by suffocation of the true self? The structures and the social conditioning to which human society is subject oppress and suffocate us all.

Misogyny: The Mother's Milk of Militarism

Society helps maintain the imprisonment of the self by other narrow sexual attitudes, such as attitudes toward homosexuality, particularly in despising male homosexuals and attributing this form of sexuality to any man who demonstrates feminine characteristics. Society subjects such "effeminate" persons to discrimination and despisement if they do not indulge in enough self-hatred to completely sublimate these characteristics and sexual preferences, or hide them. So interpreted, misogyny is not only an expected condition but in fact a form of self-hatred in which both men and women are conditioned to despise the feminine and thereby, to some degree, women (Brock-Utne, 1981).

Some social observers have identified this type of misogyny as a contemporary rather than a traditional characteristic of society. My own assessment is that the phenomenon has become more apparent owing to a growing sensitivity to the significance of these attitudes to other major social issues. However, it is enlightening to read such cogent observations as:

> It is symptomatic of the underlying tenor of American life that vulgar terms for sexual intercourse also convey the sense of getting the better of someone, working him over, taking him in, imposing

your will through guile, deception or superior force. Verbs associated with sexual pleasure have acquired more than the usual over-
tones of violence and psychic exploitation. In the violent world of
the ghetto, the language of which now pervades American society
as a whole, the violence associated with sexual intercourse is directed
with special intensity by men against women, specifically their mothers . . . all this enters everyday speech that connects sex with aggression and with highly ambivalent feelings about the mother.
(Lasch, 1979, pp. 66–67)

The objectification of women as preconditioning for militarism
is well demonstrated in a film entitled *Between Men* (Roberts, 1980),
wherein several young men recounting their experiences with the
military became conscious of this phenomenon and the degree to which
it contributed to their own dehumanization. The development of this
kind of sensitivity has arisen from consciousness-raising processes taking place in the male counterpart of the women's liberation movement,
a phenomenon described by Marc Feigen-Fasteau in his book *The Male
Machine* (1978). Feigen-Fasteau documents the negative consequences
imposed on men by rigid, stereotypic sex-role designations and indicates the degree to which they function to encourage aggression in
men while discouraging it in women. Patrick Lee, of Teachers College, Columbia University, also has hypothesized that the types of role
expectation with which boys grow up are so much more rigidly defined
and closely monitored than those of girls that the frustration level in
boys is higher, a likely cause of aggression in boys and men (P. Lee,
private communication, 1981).

The opposite side of the objectification coin is the idealization of
women, in its own way equally dehumanizing and oppressive to
women. Idealization of women is another link between sexism and
the war system and sexual conditioning for war. Christopher Lasch
(1979, p. 189) notes that chivalry was devised as a check on the exploitation of women. Chivalry, of course, called for the protection of
women from enemies and unchivalrous men, that is, those not subject to appropriate discipline or military restraints. It was also likely
a check on misogyny (which some assert also underlies chivalry). Unchecked misogyny could threaten the replenishment of the population.
And, of course, some mechanism is necessary to provide the psychic
foundations for care and responsibility for wife, children, and close
kin that patriarchy bestows on men. (Marilyn French, in her novels,
and various sociologists have observed how frequently this "sacred"
responsibility has been violated with impunity even today, as evidenced

by incest as child abuse in the United States and "dowry murder" in India.) But chivalry placed limits on the particular women whom men were obliged to idealize or extend chivalric protection to.

Today, as if bowing to the obsolescence of physical force as the major manifestation of power in a technological age, new forms of intimidation have been derived to oblige women to accommodate to the all-women-are-fair-game syndrome. Many feminists have pointed out that the so-called sexual revolution has tended to erode some of the protection against sexual exploitation formerly provided by idealization and chivalric codes. A slogan to encourage draft resistance during the Vietnam war, "Gals say yes to guys who say no," is cited by many feminists to demonstrate the degree to which the so-called sexual revolution works against the autonomy of women, for it leaves them less protected and without the options of refusal that the older, more puritanical codes of behavior offered. It also demonstrates the degree to which even extreme radicalism is not immune from the sexist bias that feeds the war system. Given my view of the relationship between sexism and the war system, I see this further objectification of women as additional evidence of the militarization of American society.

The objectification-idealization phenomenon also reveals the commonalities between sexism and racism, another exploitative component of the war system. People of non-European origins have been perceived, as have women, as chattel, subject to slavery and the whole range of other forms of exploitation. Yet they, too, have been idealized as noble savages or as possessors of mysterious wisdom or capacities beyond those of rational Western man. It often has been noted that racism serves as a fuel to the military machine; the young men of nonwhite races, in both the "democratic" Army of the United States and the colonial troops of England, France, and Belgium, have provided an inordinate percentage of the cannon fodder. Racial minorities, like women, are excluded from power and from access to official and systematic decision making about the application of coercive force.

Both objectification and idealization negate women's authentic sexuality, making it an instrument of men's sexuality. Such perception feeds the popular assumption that women represent a lower level of human development than men, and provides another rationalization for women's exclusion from the exercise of power. A number of social scientists and social commentators have asserted that it is women's exclusion from military combat and command that helps to maintain militarism and war. Although I think this assertion overlooks the links between sexism and racism and the evidence that inclusion of minorities has made it possible to extend rather than limit the power of the military, the issue is still one that deserves consideration in any examination of the links between sexism and the war system.

Miles Wolpin, a political scientist from the State University of New York at Potsdam, has hypothesized that technology has eradicated the combat significance of differences in physical strength between men and women, and therefore it is important to study "all major involvement of women in military and paramilitary conflicts." By implication he suggests that excluding women from command helps to maintain militarism.

> Sexist as well as racist discriminatory patterns and oppression are ultimately enforced by the coercive apparatus of the state. Ascriptive discrimination of women as a group from combat units and roles not only denies them equal rights but excludes them *a priori* from attaining the highest command positions within the armed forces — given the traditional requirement that top officers have combat experience. Such exclusion also insures that the military coercive state apparatus will remain a male-dominated institution. (Wolpin, 1981)

That such an issue would even be considered as a research topic is deemed by some to mark a significant success for women's progress toward equality. The equal right to serve in the military has been viewed by some, even feminists, as a major step forward. However, it also should be noted that the issue has raised profound controversy among women's groups. The traditional peace organizations feel that women's resistance to military service is a form of struggle against war and militarism. Still others believe that the presence of women in the military could serve to mitigate the savagery of warfare and contribute to some prudence in decisions to use armed forces — the presumption being that more restraint will be applied if the forces are made up equally of women and men. The restraint would stem from two fundamental sexist assumptions, namely, that women will be less prone to initiate and to escalate violence, and that men in opposing forces will be reluctant to inflict violence on women. (It must be noted that the latter assumption has proved to be true when the opposing forces are of similar cultures. But American armed forces have released the full force of military violence against Native American, Filipino, and Vietnamese women and children.) These assumptions relate closely to the complementary assertion that society is more willing to sacrifice young men than young women, a notion reinforced by Franco Fornari's work (1974). He indicates that one psychiatric theory attributes war to the desire of the adult male to do away with the upcoming young who will be contending for the exercise of power. (The desire to control and subjugate ung men is characteristic of patriarchy.) This theory, however, has received much less attention than the former idea that conscription of women into the military and into combat forces would help to erode militarism and limit the occurrence of warfare. This idea has been expressed by world order scholar Ali Mazrui (1974) and by popular historian Frances Fitzgerald (1980) who, in the *New York Times*'s op-ed page, indicated that the main reason for excluding women from the military was the fear that they would "contaminate a sacred male precinct" and effect significant change in the military.

Some who support the need for a strong defense capability still view such change as an undesirable weakening of the military in that women are physically unfit for combat and unable to perform the feats of derring-do traditionally carried out by brave young men. It also is asserted that equal numbers of women would introduce feminine values into the military, thereby softening it and eroding the masculine value of effective war-making capacity. Most especially, it is argued, women are not equipped to deal with the stress of the battlefield, even if the battlefield is the console of a computer in a highly technological war room.

The admission of women into the military also may be looked on as part of a co-optation of rather than a concession to the women's movement. One observable co-optative trend has been the masculinization of women, an attempt to let a few of them into the club, so to speak, to quiet them down and divert attention from further feminist demands. To function in the male world women must think like men, act like men, and indeed look like men. This is a trend evident in fashion advice to young women seeking to become executives. They are told to wear business suits, and carry briefcases, not purses. Looking at the cut of military uniforms for women shows how ill-adapted the female form is to military garb, and certainly military garb has been little adapted to the female form. (That military clothing is so much in fashion now is further evidence of the general militarization of society.)

Whereas the threat of being perceived as unfeminine once intimidated women and prevented most of them from attempting to enter the fields of business, the military, and the professions, now, as a consequence of having internalized the image and values of the oppressor, many women seem almost eager to adopt masculine characteristics and criteria in order to succeed. Some of these women even designate themselves feminists. Many women are willing to "do their bit for their country" by serving in the military; in fact they believe that it is in the interest of women's equality to do so.

This controversy within the women's movement over women's roles in the national defense and the appropriate relationship of feminism to the military also is reflected in the positions politically active women are taking in regard to security policy, the arms race, and disarmament issues. For example, it has been demonstrated in the United States that women legislators are less likely to vote in favor of high military appropriations than men legislators are. However, in their public statements, particularly close to election time, some women can outdo men in declaring their commitment to the "defense of our national security." Some of these same women are articulate proponents of women's rights and have campaigned for the Equal Rights Amendment. Nevertheless realizing that valor is the better part of discretion when it comes to national defense politics, very few successful women politicians have taken on the sexism-militarism issue. They have not attempted to educate the public, particularly their women constituents, about the relationships between sexism and the war system. There are some notable exceptions to this, women who have been very outspoken about militarism, poverty, racism, and their links to sexism. But these women tend to be branded as irresponsible and irrepressible, often earning themselves misogynist nicknames (such as "Battling Bella"). Such reactions show how profoundly threatening such assertions are to the established order.

The controversy is evident in the varying types of women's organizations and the different priorities they espouse. A few years ago some of the old established women's peace organizations were perceived by younger women as being antifeminist and unconcerned with women's issues. At the same time, long-standing members of such peace groups viewed feminist organizations as having little or no interest in the fundamental problems of justice and peace.

The differences between women in the antiwar movement and feminists who see sexism as the primary violence illustrate how little awareness there is of the common roots of sexism and the war system in misogynist attitudes and patriarchal structures. Both sides seem to see militarism and sexism as distinct, if related, problems, yet both problems are at base manifestations of misogyny. Militarism, which assumes that the human species is aggressive by nature and will submit to communal order only by force, arises from a view of human nature limited to masculine characteristics — the male as total paradigm for the human being (that is, "man"). Sexism is essentially a prejudice against all manifestations of the feminine.

Misogyny, whether manifested as despisement of the other or as self-hatred, is the taproot of the war system, running even deeper than the "taproot of all violence in society" that Father Richard McSorley

(1982) argues to be nuclear weapons. Misogyny is the core of both militarism and sexism, and unless it is completely torn from the social soil in which the male power structure cultivates war, there is no hope to uproot the war system.

Feminism as a Peace Force

A significant change in the women's movement seems to be developing in conjunction with the worldwide disarmament movement. Many women's organizations and groups formerly manifesting little or no concern with issues of war and peace or the arms race have been moved by the unprecedented threat of the spiraling nuclear arms race and the increased probability of nuclear warfare to articulate sentiments against the arms race and to take action to prevent a nuclear holocaust. It is in this context that more feminists are beginning to look at the sexist implications of militarization; to take note of the particularly severe consequences that militarization has had on women's rights, especially in developing countries; and to recognize the relationship between patriarchy and war.

There have been numerous conferences, journal and periodical articles, and a few books on feminism and militarism that may have begun a trend toward a convergence of women's concerns and peace issues, and could initiate a dialogue between the peace movement and the women's movement. This dialogue is critical in both senses of the word. Convergence of the two is politically essential to what world order studies have termed global transformation, and, as we shall see, each brings a usefully critical eye to the perspectives and approaches of the other. There are several manifestations of the possibilities for this convergence. The more vigorous initiatives come from the women's movements. More systematic but also more tentative efforts are slowly coming from the peace movement.

Women in the peace movement are beginning to focus on the links between masculine socialization and overemphasis on armed force to maintain national security (Brock-Utne, 1981; Reardon, 1981). Feminist antiwar slogans such as "take the toys away from the boys" indicate an awareness of how childhood social conditioning, which derives from sex-role separation, reinforces the social legitimation of men's use of force and weaponry. This slogan suggests the link between the different forms of play boys and girls are encouraged to engage in and the maintenance of sex-role stereotypes and the arms race. Boys who have enjoyed the fun and excitement of war games and toy weapons are not so likely to grow up to favor disarmament and the abolition of war. (Evidence that some do demonstrates that experience and education can change some fundamental, seemingly ingrained attitudes, and that early socialization is not irreversible.)

Feminist organizations and publications are taking note of the male chauvinist and misogynist nature of the military and the sexism inherent in world militarization. The fundamental similarities between the social structure of patriarchy and the organization of the armed forces are emphasized particularly by those feminists who acknowledge the war/threat system as the major vehicle keeping women in their place. They urge women not to accept service in the military as a path to equality, encouraging them rather to join their brothers who have resisted military service on grounds of ethics and conscience. Frequently denounced as cowardly, sissy, or effeminate, these male resisters have in fact demonstrated a reverence for life that has been traditionally ascribed to women rather than to men. They have gone a step beyond feminism to authentic humanism by extending the murder taboo to peoples beyond their own tribe/nation. Some, even more significantly, have come to recognize the other in themselves.

As women in the process of liberation have come to acknowledge the masculine in themselves (both as a positive and as a negative force), some men have acknowledged, even embraced, the feminine in themselves. Such acknowledgment of the other in ourselves is essential to the healing of the primal wound and to the concomitant process of humanization. It may well be one of the messages of the Christian injunction to love your enemy. If indeed the terrifier is within us, the healing process requires us truly to love ourselves with all our complexity and weaknesses, and both our feminine and masculine sides. This extension, this attribution of humanity to the enemy (the other), is the essential requirement needed to transcend sexism, liberate women from the ever-present possibility of rape, and free the human family from its thralldom to the war system and from the threat of annihilation posed by the nuclear arms race.

Although the connection between violence against women and the war system has not yet received widespread feminist attention, it is forming a more significant aspect of the feminist component of the disarmament movement and a smaller but conceptually significant influence within the peace research community. There is a strong possibility that this connection between violence against women and the war system will gain greater significance in the women's movement's current emphasis on equality. The presence of the threat of force, particularly potentially lethal force, always prevents authentic equality in any relationship, whether structural or interpersonal. Feminists are aware of this factor and are coming to see that equality cannot be selectively sought. As the links between racism and sexism become clearer, so too do the links between these two forms of repression and colonialism. In its contemporary form, colonialism, though challenged by nationalism, still keeps the Third World in economic subservience to the First World. Similarly, First World women, despite the franchise, have continued to be economically dependent on the men who run the economic system (Reardon, 1977b). By controlling the terms of trade and the transfer of technology, the First World continues to dominate the world economic system. By discrimination in wages and exclusion from the economic power structure, women as a group are kept in a position of subservience to men. Both instances indicate how enforced dependency operates to maintain dominance.

The desire to maintain their domination of the global economy is recognized as a major cause of militarization among the industrial nations. It is particularly interesting that this causal relationship has been most cogently illuminated in the United States by Randall Forsberg (1982), a woman peace researcher and director of the Institute for Defense and Disarmament Studies. The economic consequences of the arms race have also been most fully documented and widely disseminated by a woman economist, Ruth Sivard, director of World Priorities, Incorporated. Women's traditional concern with peace and disarmament is now being reinforced by serious and widely respected research as well as effective, hard-headed action.

Feminists are beginning to study the symbiosis Oberg has identified between the arms race and structural violence. They are particularly concerned with the impact of this condition on women and how it illuminates the more general and pervasive problems of sexism. It is especially enlightening to look at the issues in terms of development as well. Robin Burns, an Australian feminist peace researcher, observes:

> Violence, in structural terms, links underdevelopment, peacelessness and discrimination based on biological characteristics. A structurally violent situation is one in which the means for the attainment of certain rights is controlled by the group in power, removing not only power but the right to define oneself from those who are controlled. Thus:
>
> (i) *Development and peace* are reciprocally linked if peace is defined not as the absence of war but the achievement of positive social and cultural goals. The oppressive structures which limit or deform

development in the interests of the rich and powerful, trade on insecurity to justify armaments and draw ordinary people into their folly, partly through denial of alternative ideas and contacts. The violence is also seen in the amount of money spent on arms, especially when this is compared with development aid: the tying of resources to destruction and threat rather than improvement of the human lot. One particular aspect of this is the development of high technology increasingly associated with the military, and the implications of this as a "development model," as well as the tying up of one-third of the world's scientists in military and paramilitary research. (Burns, 1982)

In the peace action field, women's groups are undertaking to bring these links to public attention. The Peace People movement in Northern Ireland was launched by two women as a response to one particular violent conflict, but it took its inspiration from traditions of nonviolence that are a major source of ethical inspiration for the new abolitionists who seek to eliminate war as a legitimate institution (*New Abolitionists*, 1978).

Although some of the efforts appear to be spontaneous, in fact they represent the systematic, inevitable emergence (often sparked by desperation) of feminine private values into the masculine public sphere (Reardon, 1975c). The Women for Peace movement in Europe, the Women's Pentagon Action in the United States, and the Greenham Common women in England are good examples of public action for political purposes inspired by private and personal feminine values.

The Women for Peace movement was started by one woman, Ann Bocaccio, in Switzerland and several in Scandinavia who could no longer passively accept the ever-mounting nuclear threat. Their action took the form of a campaign to urge women all over the world to write to the leaders of the superpowers, demanding an end to the nuclear arms race. These women also organized major international peace marches, among them one to Moscow timed to arrive about the time of the U.N. Second Special Session on Disarmament (SSDII).

Through demonstrations at the Pentagon and other public actions and feminist celebrations, the Women's Pentagon Action enlisted feminists in the antimilitarist movement and raised public consciousness about the monstrous extension of machismo represented by the inordinate dedication of resources to military might. They emphasize particularly how these resource priorities continue to prevent women from having access to basic social services, health care, education, and jobs (Women's Pentagon Action, 1980).

The Greenham Common women have gained worldwide admiration for their courage, tenacity, and inventiveness. Their encampment at the site of an American cruise missile base in England has inspired similar actions around the world. Their long struggle has included, in addition to the encampment, international speaking tours and participation in demonstrations that sometimes resulted in arrests. Though their efforts did not prevent the installation of the American missiles, they have not given up. They have even proceeded to legal action, bringing a class-action suit against the president and the secretary of defense of the United States, a move that contributes as much to public education as it does to feminist inspiration.

Trends in peace research and world order studies, instigated by the reemergence of interest in the institution of war itself as a central research question, also indicate possibilities for integration of these two peace-related fields with women's studies. The previously noted insight into the relationship between structural violence and the arms race is potentially the most promising of such possibilities. Other fields of study needing further exploration to reveal their potential are women in development, which raises structural issues closely related to those inherent in the arms race; and human rights, which is generally construed as a field distinct from that of women's rights. (The Columbia University Human Rights Center is a notable exception, viewing women's rights as integral to human rights.) Authoritarianism, militarism, and militarization also provide the bases for serious consideration of patriarchy as a cause of war. Finally, the recent concern that world order studies has demonstrated for culture as a significant variable to be included in the analysis of global problems opens the way for exploration of the nature and influence of culturally embedded sexism and sexist values.

The masculinization, indeed the militarization, of women and the increase in actual and symbolic violence against them reflect a fundamental awareness of the challenges that such trends and the growth of feminism pose to partiarchy. They also constitute an obvious acknowledgment of the effectiveness of women peace activists in mobilizing new groups against violence and in support of disarmament. At a very deep level feminism is recognized as a powerful peace force — not only in the sense of the term as an intervention in a course of violence, but more significantly as a vital energy for peace. Feminism is a force for the transcendence of organized violence, violence rooted in sexism, strengthened by sexist values, and perpetuated by male-chauvinist behavior.

This peace force is the fruit of feminine values and is manifest in feminine skills. Positive feminine values are interpersonal and humane. In terms of peace values they complement and give life to the abstract, institutional world order values. I would categorize these institutional values as positive masculine values because of their form as well as their derivation. Both sets of positive values, masculine and feminine, are essential guidelines for the achievement of a truly peaceful and just social order, and both sets of negative, distorted masculine and feminine characteristics are severe impediments to peace and justice. All of the positive values are human values to be embraced and developed by both men and women. Positive masculine values have been pursued mainly by men in their public, communal roles, and positive feminine values have been sought by women in their private, family roles. Among these latter are values sorely needed in public policy making: diversity, cooperation, caring, equality, fairness, and love, the fundamental life-affirming value. Positive feminine values have been the subject of exploration in an emerging public discussion in the print and electronic media. There is no need to define and catalogue them here, but simply to observe that these values are the wellspring of most women's activism for peace and justice and a significant motivating factor for many men in the movement. They inform some of the scholarly work done by both women and men seeking to build a knowledge base for peace, particularly in that research related to positive peace. (Positive peace, the conditions of justice and equity necessary to achieve the absence of war, is a concept profoundly infused with feminine values.) But positive feminine values have yet to be given their rightful central place in the field. Neither feminine values nor the increased participation of women are a central concern of the peace movement or peace research.

Chapter 4

SEXISM AND THE PEACE SYSTEM: CRITICISM/SELF-CRITICISM

WHEN I FIRST BEGAN to explore the connections between sexism and the war system, raising the issue with peace researchers, one woman researcher suggested that a more relevant inquiry would be sexism in the peace system, meaning the peace research "establishment." The statement reflected the primary perception feminists hold of peace research, another arena from which women and women's concerns are virtually excluded. For their part peace researchers tend to see neither the exclusion nor the relevance of the issues. And so it is and has been with politicians and statesmen.

> After the war the Women's International League for Peace and Freedom (WILPF) sent a proposal to the Peace Conference in Paris in 1919 suggesting measures aimed at avoiding a new war. When Emily Greene Balch, the first Secretary General of WILPF, received the Nobel Peace Prize in 1946, the Director of the Nobel Institute, Gunnar Jahn, said: "I want to say so much that it would have been extremely wise if the proposal WILPF made to the Conference in 1919 had been accepted by the Conference. But few of the men listened to what the women had to say. The atmosphere was too bitter and revengeful. And on top of this there was the fact that the proposal was made by women. In our patriarchal world suggestions which come from women are seldom taken seriously. Sometimes it would be wise of the men to spare their condescending smiles." (Brock-Utne, 1981)

The same point could be made about the contemporary peace establishment. The gap between the women's movements and the peace movement certainly has its counterpart in the academic and research communities. This is probably a far more serious split in that it separates the theories and strategies that feminist scholarship and peace research apply to understanding and resolving conflicts that have their origins in the same fundamental causes. Thereby each field remains inadequate to the tasks of deriving truly relevant knowledge and devising effective policies. Both have become more conscious of the inadequacies of the other, but neither has acknowledged that these might be significantly reduced by a convergence of insights gained from their separate inquiries into their common concern with overcoming exploitation and violence. Feminist criticism of peace research and world order studies dwells most on the inadequacies of those fields arising from the exclusion of women and women's perspectives.

> The study of peace is as much a male activity as the making of war. Despite the fact that some few women scholars work in the field, and that women have been important peace activists, peace research expresses a male point of view.
>
> The mainstream discourse of peace research (as indicated by publications in the journals) has been characterised as divided into two camps: the quantitative-behaviouralists, and the critical peace research group. This division is slightly misleading; some of the latter play with numbers, and many of the former are attempting to quantify the same values and hopes discussed by the latter. Sharp critiques from both camps point out the necessity to study violence on the direct, personal and indirect, structural levels, although they cannot agree what violence is and how it may be recognised and measured.
>
> What stands out in this debate is the lack of recognition that violence is differently experienced and participated in, by women and men. This lack is, I would argue, causally connected to the sterility and futility of the debate.
>
> Peace studies aim to bring about peace. As Juergen Dedring has pointed out, such was the hope of the "pacifists and activists who were the godfathers [sic] of peace research." Research alone is useless; there must be the "opportunity to influence men [sic] and events."
>
> This lack of influence is not surprising considering peace studies' naivete about power. Berenice Carroll in 1972 published a superb critique of the inadequacy of the concepts of power and dangers of the "cult of power" in peace studies. Apparently no one was listening: these issues and concepts have not been taken up in journals. In accusing peace researchers of naivete about power, I mean power in general, and men's positions and interests in the world in particular. Power is exercised along gender as well as class lines; it is usually men who exercise power. (Roberts, 1982)

For its part a world order and peace research critique of feminism would emphasize its failure to give adequate attention to the major systematic and structural inequities that hold virtually all oppressive systems in place.

Self-Criticism:
Feminism's Limited Approach to War

My own critique of contemporary North American mainstream feminism as a political movement as well as a field of study focuses primarily on its lack of structural considerations. This, in turn, seems to impose some serious perspective limitations on the feminist approach to war and the war system.

The primary limitations that world order analysts would attribute to feminist perspectives, as applied to social, economic, and political problems, especially problems of violence, are a lack of structural analysis and insufficient attention to the characteristics of the overall system. As the purpose of world order studies is to analyze systems in terms of their capacities to achieve values, world order advocates would say that feminists cannot produce a valid or adequate diagnosis of the fundamental problems unless they analyze the structural, systemic foundations.

One example of this limited perspective was the International Tribunal on Crimes Against Women, which was held in Belgium in 1976. This tribunal has much to recommend it as an event contributing toward raising public awareness about the oppression of women: first, in specifying and documenting those forms of violence that could be categorized as crimes against women; second, as "a major accomplishment in breaking through nationalisms: women of the world uniting to oppose patriarchy everywhere." The official report of the tribunal, however, makes little or no recognition of either militarization or the economic control exercised by multinational corporations as major causes of women's oppression. It makes no reference at all to political or economic structures. This document seems to me to have been drafted in a very narrow frame of reference, particularly its attribution of blame solely to patriarchy in its traditional form without acknowledging its present manifestations in militarism and neocolonialism. One of the strongest statements in the report, while indicating a certain degree of transcendence of male-dominated international politics, also, I believe, reflects this narrowness of focus.

For example, the Israeli participants proposed that "the dialogue between Arab and Jewish women that has begun at this tribunal shall continue within the framework of international feminism. As women we understand that our oppression is by men and not by opposing nationalities. The Tribunal is the first international forum in which both Israeli and Arab women have each publicly condemned their own societies for their oppression against women rather than condemning one another. (International Tribunal on Crimes Against Women, 1976)

I sincerely doubt that such a statement would have been made by most Arab women, who, the changes in world power balance notwithstanding, still see themselves as oppressed more by Western imperialism than by their own men. As women of the Third World they know that all people in their society, both men and women, are oppressed. Although women in these societies are certainly more oppressed, their oppression is part of a total system that such Western feminist analysis has not taken sufficiently into account. Indeed, to assert "that our oppression is by men and not by opposing nationalities" not only ignores the structures that enforce sexist oppression and contemporary economic paternalism, but also attributes to nation-states a degree of autonomy they simply do not have. This reinforces the myth of sovereignty, which is another significant support of the war system. The assertion also fails to challenge the nation-state itself and all related international structures as essentially patriarchal.

A lack of structural analysis cannot, however, be attributed to Marxist feminists or to some Third World feminists. Many of these women scholars would not identify themselves as feminists because they see women's liberation as only one component of a wider global political struggle for liberation. It is not only a struggle against domestic confinement in the home and other forms of purdah, but also and foremost a struggle against the oppressive economic structures of imperialism, particularly capitalist imperialism. Some women scholars even reject the concept of patriarchy as a cause of sexist oppression, attributing it more to capitalist imperialism. This was the case at the International Symposium on Women's Political Participation sponsored by the Consortium on Peace Research, Education and Development (COPRED, 1978b).

The attribution of sexism to capitalist imperialism ignores the fact pointed out by Christopher Lasch (1979, p. 206), among others, that sexism has existed in many forms throughout human history and cannot be attributed only to capitalism. Even Nancy Chodorow, in an interview about her research on gender, admitted that although her work was "an attempt to create Marxist feminist theory . . . we need more than analysis of capitalism to understand male domination" (Thurman, 1982). It could be argued that a macro-historical feminist approach reveals that Marxism, too, derives from patriarchy.

As asserted in the organizers' report of the COPRED colloquium, the apparent conflict between the two feminist perspectives — one emphasizing patriarchy, the other imperialism — serves as an obstacle to women's movements becoming a truly effective force in the global transformation process (COPRED, 1978a). For it is in the universality of women's oppression and the cross-cultural commonality of feminine values that the real potential of feminism as a peace force and a transforming power lies. A force that is to effect significant change on a global scale needs to be rooted in a global phenomenon; it must derive from a value base that is common to most human cultures. The fundamental positive feminine values are probably the most universal of any set of human values.

Another fragmenting and limiting tendency of some feminist work is the centrality given to women's concerns, separating them from other political and social problems. Certainly, any feminist analysis would require that problems be viewed from a women's perspective. Granted, the specific effects problems have on women should be studied as a fundamental aspect of the diagnosis of any problem of public policy. But a diagnosis that is only concerned with one interest group, even when that particular interest group constitutes half the human species, may do a disservice to the interests of other involved groups. Such exclusion certainly has had a negative impact on women, particularly in public policy areas related to economic and social questions and especially in the field of development. If the larger goal is research and political action for a more humane world society, then clearly the impacts on and the values of as many groups as are concerned with an issue need to be taken into account. Conflicts of interest and values must at least be considered, if not resolved. For example, many Euro-American feminists are perceived by Marxist and Third World feminists as being themselves part of the problem, because they fail to challenge the global political and economic structures that oppress the Third World. Their refusal to accept capitalism as the major oppressing force and to analyze women's oppression as a class problem is a point of contention with Marxist feminists. Unless some resolution can be reached, such perceived conflicts of interest can be a serious obstacle to the achievement of the preferred worlds of all concerned.

Certainly, they will slow progress in transcending the general system of oppression.

Here, however, it must be observed that such perception of separate interest is at once a commonly experienced stage in the "conscientization" of most oppressed groups and a necessary, though not sufficient, component of the analysis of any case of oppression. The oppressed must perceive fully and clearly how their own interests are distinct from those of the dominant group. They must also comprehend the invariable consequences of the continued suppression and camouflaging of the conflict between the oppressor and the oppressed by the accepted social norms and the dominant political and economic institutions.

The actual experience of women in the peace movement (relegation to making the coffee, "manning" the mimeograph machine, and providing sexual solace for "the activists") and the failure of the peace movement to see the relevance and relationship of women's oppression to the war system are two sound reasons for separatism. The Vietnam experience is a case in point.

> As a matter of historical record, by the time the Winter Soldier Investigation had been convened, the feminist movement and the antiwar movement had gone their separate and distinct ways, each absorbed with its own issues to the exclusion of the other, with no small amount of bitterness among movement troopers whose energies, ideologies and sense of priority pulled them in one direction or another. As a woman totally committed to the feminist cause I received several requests during this time to march, speak and "bring out my sisters" to anti-war demonstrations "to show women's liberation solidarity with the peace movement," and my response was that if the peace movement cared to raise the issue of rape and prostitution in Vietnam, I would certainly join in. This was met with strong silence on the part of anti-war activists whose catch words of the day were "anti-imperialism" and "American aggression," and from whom the slogan—it appeared on buttons—"Stop the Rape of Vietnam" meant defoliation of crops, not the abuse of women. Communications between feminist groups and anti-war groups were tense as they sought to raise our consciousness and we sought to raise our own. I am sorry that the peace movement did not consider the abuse of women in Vietnam an issue important and distinct enough to stand on its own merits, and I am sorry that we in the women's movement, struggling to find our independent voices, could not call attention to this women's side of the war by ourselves. The time was not right. (Brownmiller, 1976, p. 112)

There is little wonder that Brownmiller did not devote more time to the systemic and structural relationships between rape and the war system. (Her chapter on war deals with it as circumstance rather than system.) But one is given pause by the lack of such connections in the fields of peace research and world order studies, which are so preoccupied with structural analysis and systems approaches. The critique of this separatism leveled at feminism by both the peace researchers/ world order scholars and peace movement activists might well be tempered by a sensitivity to the consciousness-raising process and to the subjective experience of oppression. There is no better way to fixate a stage of development than to respond to it as a permanent characteristic. Neither is there a more effective way to reinforce separatism than to accept the analysis of distinct interests as sufficient and to use this as the basis of exclusion from consideration in the overall systemic analysis of the problems at issue. In fact, it was the acceptance of women's issues as separate that frequently prevented their inclusion in research and policy making.

This interplay between limited feminist analysis of the war system and the exclusion of even that limited analysis from most research and policy discussions perpetuates the same masculine exclusion of the feminine from peace research and world order studies as it has from the traditional social sciences and virtually all institutions of authority and legitimation. This exclusion in turn leads to an even more negative trend among some feminists who interpret feminism as seeking equal advantage for women. Seeking equal advantage places the emphasis on advantage, and in essence buys into the system of advantaged and disadvantaged. Policies and strategies tend to concentrate on how to move more women from the latter into the former category.

Such policies and strategies encourage women to seek success within the dominant structures characterized by masculine values and behaviors. Thus many "feminists" even in the academic, research, and social change fields have accommodated to the dominant masculine value structure. Indeed, business and professional women are encouraged to do so by some women's magazines and special training workshops that teach them how to "dress for success" and how to behave "more professionally." Most such instruction is based on a not-too-subtle process of masculinization, including wearing business suits and partaking in "completely objective" decision making. These behaviors call forth understandable criticism from many feminists as reinforcing the present system, which peace researchers and world order scholars assume to be in need of total transformation. Unfortunately for both feminism and transformation, among those few women who have gained real power status in boardrooms, in the professions, and at the highest levels of state are too many examples of such masculinization who serve as oft-quoted evidence that women in power would be no different from men.

The presence of this success syndrome in the Euro-American women's movement is a significant impediment to the realization of the transformational potential of feminism, for it is but another manifestation of the feminine personal view. It may be harder for women to perceive themselves as members of a class or as representatives of an abstract group because they are socialized to see things in personal terms and view people as persons rather than as components of abstract categories. It also must be recognized that the women most involved in the success syndrome come from the culture and class that has most isolated women from each other: the Western industrial middle class that populates suburban communities and modern cities around the world. Any group identity of such women is as likely to be with that of the successful men in their particular socioeconomic class or culture as with women of other groups.

This is not to say that women do not identify closely with others. Indeed, because of their socialization to care for others, they are more prone to do so than men. As noted, women tend to identify with others as persons, not abstract groups or classes, and with particular human experiences such as bereavement, joy, motherhood, illness, and so on. One suspects, for example, that this personal human view led the white women of the southern United States to accept, encourage, and cooperate with the Civil Rights movement before the "liberal" men. Most probably, this personal view is also what now motivates so many women into active mobilizing roles in the movement for peace and disarmament. It certainly accounts for a very particular difference between feminist studies and world order scholarship. But it must be recognized at the same time that the personal view permits liberated women to engage in a drive for individual success and personal fulfillment without regard to the effects of this drive on women in general and on the total social system.

Criticism: Peace Research as Another Male Preserve

Whereas feminism may be lacking in structural analysis, peace research has suffered several analytic shortcomings, as Roberts (1982) points out. Both peace research and world order studies have been sorely lacking in the personal, the particularly human dimension of analysis and prescription. This is clearly evident in the minimal consideration given to women's issues and women's movements and in the failure heretofore to include sexism as a problem for research and analysis.

A more obvious and more serious exclusion is that of much of the relevant work women have done in peace research and of the participation of women themselves. Peace researchers, like other professionals, are always hard put to think of more than one or two qualified women to participate in or contribute to any scholarly endeavor. Qualified, of course, means conforming to masculine standards of professional competence, that is, having passed the appropriate masculine success tests. So it is that few women, and fewer feminists, have been read or heard, much less attended to, in research and policy discourse. In the arms and militarization field this is especially lamentable, for nowhere are fresh views and new voices more urgently needed. Women such as Randall Forsberg, Ruth Sivard, Helen Caldicott, and all those women who have organized and contributed to the activism of European Women for Peace, the Mobilization for Survival, the Campaign for Nuclear Disarmament, and the Greenham Common women have demonstrated both the vision and the power required to become a force for peace.

That women do have a unique contribution to make in the area of disarmament research was illustrated in a survey conducted for the *Women's International Feminist Quarterly*. Forty-one women involved in research and scholarly writing related to peace were asked, among other questions, if they believed women have a distinct perspective on disarmament.

> Only twenty of the 41 answered the question whether women approached disarmament in distinctive ways. Several were clearly irritated by the question and all, no matter how they answered the question, felt they had earned the right to be thought of as scholars, not women who were scholars. Nine gave an unequivocal "no" to the question; of these, two said education erases gender differences. Several mentioned hardliner women colleagues and pointed out this was the way to succeed in the field. On the other hand, six thought there were differences, and five thought there might be differences, for a total of 11, thus dividing the respondents fairly evenly into pros and cons. The "maybe's" have a marginal status, tend to get less absorbed in the excitement of the power game, and on the whole appear more objective. In meetings and conferences their interventions are said to be more to the point, less embroidered with

rhetoric. Those who had a clear feminist perspective saw women as having developed different skills and different sensitivities because of their social roles as women, and therefore more likely to "humanize" the data they worked with, attempting more interpretation, trying for more reality testing. They felt that women were more inclined to see the interconnections between militarization, violence, and other features of social institutions. They would be more aware of the "ridiculousness of the intense preoccupation with military superiority" as one puts it. (Boulding, 1981)

Related research currently being undertaken by Barbara Stanford reveals that women frequently raise questions of consequences on arms policy not considered by the male policy makers or peace researchers.

Some of the real dangers of the exclusion of women's and especially feminist perspectives from peace research and education were highlighted in testimony on proposals for the National Peace Academy:

> It appears, however, that most of the Commission, Staff and Supporters are nearly strangers to most of the perspectives and insights that guide and inspire others and me in addressing and organizing for many integral dynamics of genuine peace and conflict resolution. Those guiding insights are not only but are especially feminist in philosophies, ethics and potential. No euphemisms for feminism will do; to avoid and/or devalue or marginalize the concepts, values and language of feminism would mean to be deprived of the insights, benefits and processes of this transformative and profound movement. Clearly, feminism is radical which literally means acknowledging and addressing problem-solving, in these instances, creating peace and conflict resolution. It is a basic premise of this testimony that sexism in its multiple personal and institutionalized forms throughout many societies is a (not the only) very *root* cause of violence of all kinds. (Heide, 1980)

This was a classic example of the invisibility of women to the analysts and planners. Although the Women's Decade has made the invisibility problem more evident in the field of development planning, it seems not to have enlightened most areas of research and scholarship that deal with politics. Most especially, those areas that deal with military and security issues have been almost as impervious to the invisibility-and-consequent-exclusion syndrome as the established order has been consciously determined to keep women's concerns totally separate from hard security issues (Reardon, 1975b). It has been reported that when

Scandinavian women presented disarmament petitions with thousands of signatures to U.N. officials at the Copenhagen conference to mark the midpoint of the International Women's Decade in 1980, the response was, more or less, "Congratulations and thank you very much, ladies. Now let's get back to the real business of the conference."

World Order Inquiry:
Whose Preferred World?

There are some very colorful examples of the mind-set that underlies the invisibility-exclusion syndrome. Examples include one peace researcher's insistence that concern with women's oppression was distracting attention from the more substantive and pressing problems of peace and another's assertion that it was not a problem worthy of consideration because his wife was not oppressed. These examples may seem frivolous, but they reflect a condition for which there is ample relevant evidence of the absence of women's issues and, indeed, the limited representation of women authors in peace and world order studies. If, as the male scholars assert, the data have been derived and published as a scholarly contribution toward the planning and pursuit of a preferred world, where and how are women's preferences taken into account? This question has been raised continually since at least 1975 and has yet to receive serious attention (Reardon, 1975a). While world order inquiry has confronted the disparity in the perspectives, value priorities, and political preferences between the First and Third Worlds, and at least taken into account the conflicting interests of East and West, the conflict of interest between men and women resulting from women's oppression has been ignored.

Of twenty-six papers in the World Order Working Papers series, two have been written by women. Yet however limited the representation of women among participants in publications and research conferences, exclusion of substantive women's issues is even more significant. Not one of these papers includes women's issues, much less a feminist perspective, in either the problem analysis or the policy recommendations. Although Robert Johansen in one of his essays lists women's movements among those capable of contributing to the transformation process (Johansen, 1978b), even he does not observe the special relevance of women's oppression to the problems calling for transformation. Even the most adamant feminist peace researcher could not expect sexism to be raised in every world order monograph, or even to be treated in any depth. In several, however, the complete omission of any consideration is not only exclusionary, it weakens the potential of the analysis to contribute effective recommendations regarding the transformation process.

In his otherwise excellent essay on authoritarian tendencies, Richard Falk (1980) makes no reference to the regression in the status of women that inevitably accompanies the rise of authoritarianism. In his later essay on demilitarization (1981), the omission of these factors in light of the more widespread articulation of the significant link between sexism and militarism is truly unfortunate. His very constructive suggestions on initiatives would have benefited greatly by including the necessity to transcend sexism in any authentic process of demilitarization. With one paragraph he could have made clear the relation of every person on earth to the demilitarization process and focused on an issue that is manifest in all three systems he discusses (the nation-state, the United Nations, and the global change movement) and on all scales from global to individual. Only issues of such truly comprehensive nature can serve as the real foundation of a global transformation movement.

World order, even more than other approaches to peace research, tends to be focused on issues that require a global analysis. From this, among other reasons, it might be expected that world order advocates would include feminist perspectives and demonstrate concern for sexism; but this is not the case. The invisibility of sexism is a serious blind spot, blotting out the most universal aspect of a system in need of transformation.

Another otherwise excellent working paper is a cogent example of the tendency toward blindness to certain universals and exclusion by omission. Gernot Kohler's *Global Apartheid* (1979) frustrates the expectation that world order scholars would show concern for these issues. Yet at the same time, paradoxically, it offers a very promising paradigm for feminist global analysis. Kohler's analysis of the entire international order as a system of apartheid dividing the world into advantaged and disadvantaged is applicable, as well, to the sexist values and structures that impose sex-role separation. The same analysis could be made of the sex-role separation system as that applied to the global apartheid system in the economic, social, and political spheres. A similar paradigm, of course, explicates most systems of oppression, all forms of racism, colonialism, and various manifestations of economic oppression (Reardon, 1977a). The fundamental paradigm encompassing the common characteristics of oppression as manifested in these phenomena has not been applied by world order research to the problem of sexism. Even Kohler in this most comprehensive analysis does not acknowledge the analogy to sexism. What makes this especially lamentable is that sexism offers the possibility of analyzing not only the structural aspects of the social, economic, and political characteristics of oppression, but like racism it provides the basis for cultural and psychosocial analysis as well. In addition, it offers the aforementioned element of universality, which would make the analysis relevant to virtually everyone on Earth. Yet sexism is not selected for the condemnation that racial and economic apartheid is, much less mentioned in most of the litanies against oppression.

There is reason to suspect that it is precisely because of its universality that it is ignored. For once sexism is recognized, even those of us who put forth the diagnosis acknowledging sexism as the tap root of oppression will have to acknowledge our own need to take part in the prescriptional process. Like the Orwellian equal pigs, we who live in a sexist society are all sexist, though some are more sexist than others. Not only will we have to admit our own acquiescence, if not to the system, at least to its norms and its manifestations, but also, if we are truly committed to transformation, we, too, will have to change. This means giving up some control. As with the much denounced nation-state, it means relinquishing certain aspects of personal sovereignty and control over others, a process that comes especially hard to the masculine mind, whether it resides in a male or a female body.

The Cartesian Trap:
The Fundamental Sexism of the Social Sciences

The masculine mind tends to reject the sphere of feeling, and masculine sciences denigrate emotionalism. Personal change requires confrontation of feelings and the emotional components of the situation to be changed. Although there is some recognition that political change requires behavioral change, the masculine scientific approach even manages to depersonalize this process, to obscure it with the objective analysis of the social sciences. The masculine mind, which has been socialized into sublimating and suppressing emotions, particularly the softer feminine feelings, prefers to deal with this aspect of social and human experience by professionalizing it into scientific form, such as psychiatry and sociology. World order insists on the consideration of values, but, like its parent disciplines, avoids the true seat of value formation, that which educators call the affective domain. This is the world of feelings: the world in which sexism festers most and inflicts the deepest pain, the world in which the roots of the war system are continually cultivated by suppressing half of all human values and oppressing half of the human species.

I cannot believe that many peace researchers understand the feelings of women scholars when they see publication after publication containing no women's names, or a few tokens, or when they view photograph after photograph of all-male meetings (the women sometimes appear in pictures of the cocktail receptions). The intense feeling of exclusion and rejection always gives rise to the question "Whose preferred world do world order studies seek?" Like the bar in the Princeton Club (and other strongholds of power that have excluded women), it appears to us that the threshholds of the futures projected by world order scholars are also engraved "where women cease to trouble."

I do not believe that the male governmental delegates who sat with emotionless faces on the dying day of the Second Special Session on Disarmament in July 1982 truly could have understood the tears shed during those same hours by the women volunteers tending the Plowshares Coffee House across the street from the U.N. Run by women like those of Greenham Common, the Coffee House was a center for the nongovernmental peace workers who had come to observe and, if possible, to influence that special session of the General Assembly.

In the name of scholarship, world order in particular and peace research in general have steered clear (despite protestations of intellectual radicalism) of digging into the fundamental root causes of war, which certainly "begins in the minds of men" (and no feminist peace researcher would seek to change that wording). Both world order and peace research seem to have gone along with the symptomatic, reductionist approach that declares the need to treat the illness and try to halt the spread of the infection but does not necessarily conduct a true pathological or etiological investigation. Research into causes seems to be limited to overt political and economic structures and systems, omitting the inner psychic structures.

Even the profoundly significant work on the subject, such as the previously mentioned analyses by psychiatrist Franco Fornari, is given little or no consideration. The insights and contributions of psychiatrists Jerome Frank, Judd Marmor, and the few who published on the topic in the 1960s were given little attention by researchers, even during the days when such ideas were in intellectual vogue.

The resurgence of interest in psychological perspectives on the arms race is owed primarily to the antinuclear movement. And if any scientific field is to be credited with this development it is medicine. The psychiatrists themselves have put forth their contributions within the context of the physicians' movement, and some of them, particularly Robert J. Lifton, have come tantalizingly close to exposing the raw center of the human psyche from which war and violence come forth. Yet none of these recent works has given any serious attention to the significant possibilities for understanding and policy response that lie in feminist scholarship. Given the nature of the nuclear threat, a preoccupation with the arms race and impending annihilation rather than with the institution of war and the promise of transformation is understandable. However, the focus of concern is still primarily structural and disturbingly phallic, for the preoccupation is more with the weapons themselves than with the fundamental causes.

Attention to the personal and behavioral has been sorely lacking. This may be why, despite elaborate models and inspired visions of preferred worlds, we have no sound, workable transition strategies; why we have no clearly marked route "from here to there." It also may be why there are still such strong contradictions between our behaviors, our actual lived lives, and the world order values we articulate. Why is it seemingly so much easier to apply these values to political analysis than to personal behavior? Why, indeed, do we acknowledge sexism as a social problem but remain reluctant to admit to it in ourselves? Most probably it is because we know how deep it lies within our very beings that we are reluctant to put it on our professional agendas. What we seek to avoid is the scorn of our colleagues in the scholarly mainstream whose scientific standards we purport to observe and uphold, so as to legitimate and validate our field as a science (at least a social science, though those are admittedly softer, that is, feminine disciplines).

The war system has brought us to the brink of annihilation, and we still refuse to face the very fundamental feeling it arouses—fear. The society is paralyzed by the masculine suppression of emotion. Surely peace research and world order studies should attend to this paralysis as the first priority in transition. Yet for the most part we continue to close out the world of feeling and the repositories of that world, feminine values and women.

The male chauvinist bias of the field was, however, inevitable, given the intellectual formation of the researchers and the environments in which the research is pursued. Academia, like all institutional power bases, is profoundly and scandalously sexist. And on the "academic farm" the sciences, both natural and social, are somewhat more sexist than other disciplines. The social sciences, in which some semblance of ethical and human concerns might have been expected to wield some influence, have gone to extremes to prove themselves as sciences. Concerns that carry feminist values or perspectives, although sometimes considered, are given very low priority and seem to be something of an embarrassment, particularly when natural scientists deride the scientific pretensions of the social scientists. Peace researchers and educators in their attempts to gain a foothold in the scholarly community, sometimes have tried to be "more quantitative than thou." Even world order inquiry, with its avowedly normative perspective and value orientation, has gone to great lengths to establish its scholarly credentials. These circumstances, for a whole host of reasons, a number of them discussed in earlier sections of this essay, militate against feminine influence and women's participation. They probably also account for the weapons counting approach to disarmament research and education, which Norwegian feminist/scholar Birgit Brock-Utne (personal communication, 1982) sees as posing a significant antifeminine bias in that particular field. And they are even brought into play to excuse and rationalize male chauvinist behaviors among peace researchers.

These circumstances, though they may be inevitable, are not irremediable. They must be reviewed and amended openly, not only because they perpetuate sexism in peace research, but most especially because they prevent peace researchers from producing and applying transformational knowledge. Such circumstances are not excusable, having been brought up to researchers on many occasions over the last decade by many critics of the Western intellectual establishment. One of the most relevant and cogent of these critiques comes from the feminist futurist Hazel Henderson (1978), who has referred to the sterile rationalism of the social sciences as the Cartesian trap, a nice abridgment of the whole culture and mind set.

In an argument reminiscent of Garcia Chafardet's about the distortion of masculinity and femininity inherent in sex role separation, Douglas Sloan (1983) asserts that the distortion of science — scientism, resulting from its separation from human and ethical concerns — is in large part responsible for the development of our present nuclear peril. The dualism it has fostered has tended to fractionate knowledge, fragment experience, and denigrate the intuitive and imaginative capacities we need so desperately at this juncture. These latter traits are fundamental feminine elements forced out of intellectual and political discourse by masculine rationalism and reductionism. Although this mind set still controls the flow of the scientific mainstream, there are some refreshing contemporary currents from which we can take hope.

Since at least the beginning of the twentieth century, much has happened within science that calls into question the exclusively reduc-
tionistic, mechanistic, and objectivistic understanding of reality that
nineteenth century scientific assumptions seemed in so many ways
to support. Increasingly in this century, the data generated in scientific inquiry, the interpretive frameworks employed to make sense
of the data, and the understanding by scientists of their own methods
of inquiry have all become less and less congenial to a worldview
reared exclusively on a positivistic foundation. (Sloan, 1983, p. 91)

It has long been my belief that world order inquiry is just such an interpretive framework. Its scholars have attempted to be more holistic
than those in other world affairs studies; they aspire to the identification of universal human values; and, at least at the level of articulation, they abjure male chauvinism. As a woman I have often felt un-
comfortable in the male-dominated settings of world order inquiry.
As a feminist, however, I have always been comfortable, if not satisfied, with the world order framework. For me it works to explicate
most of the structural, skeletal issues of the global social order; feminism serves to flesh out the inquiry, to give it the human, living dimension sought by all global humanists. And I would place most world
order scholars and most feminist peace researchers in that category.
        However, the goals of global humanism, the world order move-
ment, and universal feminism all require that the fundamental sexism of our intellectual tools and our political strategies be confronted
and transcended. Feminism has begun to challenge the political structures; it must also challenge all intellectual paradigms. Virtually every
paradigm, every discipline, and every mode of inquiry is based on
the model of masculinity as human: the male as the norm for human
development — personally, socially, and intellectually. Our intellectual
tools, therefore, are inadequate and inhumane and need to be rede-
signed according to a balanced, fully human model of the person. This
redesign task is as much the responsibility of peace research and world
order studies as it is of feminism.
        Parts of the immediately foregoing paragraphs are particularly
feminine, yet not fully. The feminine and therefore feminist approaches
would be more personalized and concentrate more on specific behaviors, attributing the problems more to persons and behaviors than to
structures and disciplines. My hunch is that a mix of the structural
and personal approaches is required and without equal consideration
of both we will not be able to move back from the brink of annihila-

tion. It seems to me, too, that the onus falls on advocates of world order studies and peace research.

Neither women in general nor feminists in particular have rejected the significance of war as the major threat to survival. Although some see the liberation of women as a necessary first, but not necessarily simultaneous, step toward the abolition of war, there have been no outright refusals from feminists to consider the other issue, and the exploration of the connections is at last underway among feminist scholars. But the lion has ignored or refused the overtures of the lamb.

Some of the Lion's Share for the Lamb:
Resources for Feminist Peace Research

The lion-lamb metaphor is relevant to the issues of masculinity-femininity and dominance-dependence and to the questions of power, which, Roberts (1982) reminds us, Berenice Carroll tried to bring to the attention of the peace research community a decade ago. The male researchers, inventors of *polemology*, the study of war, are unquestionably the monarchs of the polemological jungle. In their attitudes and behaviors toward feminism and feminine concerns they have displayed the range of dominant male leonine behavior. The feminine lambs have recently ceased to be so meek. They have attempted to transfer the gentleness of their concerns to their professional endeavors, but by virtue of the system they have continued to remain dependent. Actually, what is advocated here is as pragmatically necessary to the millennial transformation, the achievement of authentic peace, as is the general comprehension of the full meaning of the biblical passage. The dominant and the dependent both need to accept and actualize their mutual interdependence, for purposes of survival and community building.

The foundation of community is the sharing of power and resources. Peace research and world order studies, still not fully accepted in the academic and scientific mainstream and certainly underfunded, are far better established than women's studies, especially that small minority concerned with the sexism-militarism link. They are also far better financed than any women's endeavors, except some that deal with women and development or integrating women into corporate and professional structures. The two major supports they could give to women and women's concerns (that is, attention and funding) have yet to be offered. Sexism has not even made it into the peace research journals, much less the programs of either the International Peace Research Association (IPRA) or the World Order Models Project (WOMP). IPRA has sanctioned study groups, and small groups have organized from time to time to deal with sexism within the association; both IPRA and WOMP held panels in observation of International Women's Year in 1975; but the issues have not been seriously integrated into research agendas, publication schedules, or conferences and seminars. A first step toward the kind of research integration advocated here has been taken by IPRA's Peace Education Commission (PEC), which established a study group on women and militarism and other aspects of violence against women. I hope that WOMP's initial sponsorship of this present work also represents a step toward sustained, serious consideration of the issues on the part of that particular group of scholars.

The real test of commitment is, of course, allocation of resources. Some funding was granted by UNESCO to initiate the IPRA-PEC endeavor with a research consultation. But IPRA and WOMP have yet to attempt to raise funds for such research. (It should be acknowledged that IPRA did facilitate the establishment of the African Women's Association for Research and Development.) It is, in the last analysis, this literal lack of support that has caused some feminist peace researchers to give up on the masculine establishment and seek their own way, opting for the poverty of self-reliance rather than that of dependence. It is possible that self-reliance may be the better way at the early stages of feminist peace research, but an indefinite period of separatism can only delay the urgently needed convergence.

Chapter 5

TRANSFORMATION AND TRANSITION: TOWARD CONVERGENCE

AMONG THE CRITICISMS colleagues provided on earlier drafts of this monograph, two were especially sharp and frequent. First was the expression of disappointment at the absence of a blueprint for change. Second and more disturbing was the observation of how depressing the readers found the analysis. Because my argument was both convincing and overwhelming, some said, the depth and pervasiveness of the problem made them despair of significant progress toward resolution. The criticism surprised me. The reflections laid out here have been a kind of "Eureka" experience, an insight into transformational possibilities. In finally coming to see some of the reasons why the problem of war has been so continuous and universal, I feel more hopeful of the possibility that solutions can be developed. Granted, the specific modes and avenues to resolution are far from clear. However, the intention of this monograph was to introduce the notion of the deep-rooted connections between sexism and the war system, to encourage further reflection and research, and to suggest some directions for response to these insights. Beyond the limited suggestions offered here, further elaboration of strategies for change is certainly called for.

Personal Notions of the Transformation Process

On reflection it occurs to me that my surprise at these criticisms was in large part a product of my own notions of transformation and transition which, it seems, combine both feminist and world order perspectives.

For me transformation involves a profound cultural change of such consequence and dimension as to constitute a different world. Social and political institutions certainly would have to be changed radically, but, more significantly, so too would human relations, both social and personal. My preferred future is one without sexism or racism, which among other attributes of the present I hope to see banished from that different world. This would mean a very different way of relating to others, even for those very few who had not in pretransformation days been afflicted with those particular social diseases.

Structural design certainly figures into my notion of transformation, but its role in the total change process is secondary to that of significant changes in human relations. The fundamental values of equity and mutuality, which I advocate as the norms to guide the changes, would of necessity also influence social and political structures. The structural changes, however, should emerge from the changing relations rather than coming prior to them. In other words, structures should facilitate human relations and give institutional form to the fundamental values rather than dictate and control relations and values as they have in male-dominated society. Thus a blueprint is not part of these reflections on the question of transformation. The emphasis here is more on the need for personal and relational change. If we cannot change ourselves, I doubt we can change the world.

In this context transition strategies are means by which personal and relational changes are translated into social movement and political action. The personal and the political are thoroughly intertwined in the present reality and therefore cannot be divided neatly into two distinct separate arenas for change in any transition plan that purports to be headed toward genuine transformation. This intertwining of the personal and the political makes education, viewed as the process by which we learn new ways of thinking and behaving, a very significant component of the transition-transformation processes. Education is that process through which we glimpse what might be and what we ourselves can become. It is also the process through which we articulate what might be and through which we strive to become what we choose to be. Through it we learn to choose and to pursue choices. Education is transformative when it produces visions to be pursued (that is, the goal of the *transformation*) and when it develops the capacities to achieve the goal (that is, *transition* skills, the strategies for struggle).

Static Structural
Versus Living Organic Notions of Transformation

The fundamental normative notions of transformation and transition that characterize world order studies have held a special attraction for those of us who see education as the most significant component of the struggle for peace and justice. Education is an affirmation of the human capacity to change, learn, and mature. Yet the application and articulation of those notions have always fallen far short of their full transformative potential, expressed, as they have been in most of the world order literature, in primarily mechanistic linear terms. Purportedly normative, the field has paid little attention to human behaviors and human emotions, focusing primarily on political phenomena and structural issues.

It has long been my belief that authentic transformation of the global order is as much a matter of emotional maturity as of structural change. The crux of the argument set forth in this book, that neither sexism nor the war system can be overcome independently from the other, lies in the assumption that structural, even revolutionary, changes in the public order without significant inner psychic changes in human beings will be ineffective, old wine in new bottles (Reardon, 1980). This indeed is the lesson we learn from a long history of revolutions. Authentic transformations have occurred only when people themselves have changed their world views, their values, and their behaviors as a basis for change in the social and political structures. Such changes usually involve the society coming to perceive itself as a manifestation of a new set of human, sometimes cosmic, relationships. This assumption about the interrelationship of personal and political change, which has been a major influence on my approach to peace education, began as an intuition but has evolved into a fundamental hypothesis, one that is shared by other feminists.[3]

This hypothesis is what lies at the base of feminist insistence that the personal circumstances of women have political roots and political significance. It is central to what some have perceived as an inordinate feminist emphasis on specific details of personal relationships between men and women and preoccupation with domestic social and economic policies that affect the everyday quality of life for women. Child care, abortion rights, and payment for housework, although conceptualized and expressed in terms of improving women's lot, are at base as structural as the concerns with such issues as peace-keeping forces and adjudication procedures that world order models have emphasized.

Such feminist proposals integrated into our concepts of transformation and transition could introduce into world order studies no-

---

3. Among other works that reflect the significance of the relationship between personal change and political change, see the work of J. B. Elshtain, especially *Public man, private woman* (Princeton, NJ: Princeton University Press, 1981). See also J. B. Miller, *Toward a new psychology of women* (Boston: Beacon Press, 1976) and R. Morgan, *The anatomy of freedom* (New York: Anchor Press/Doubleday, 1982).

tions of the human and quotidian, the everyday lived experience of ordinary people, to which most people can relate more readily. It is at least one approach to overcoming the commonly held perception that world order models and peace research proposals lack relevance to the real world. It is, in fact, this lack of human detail that gives the pejorative connotation to the criticism that such academic visions of a peaceful and just world system are utopian. Feminist utopias provide flesh and bone, human and quotidian dimensions that enable us to catch a glimpse of what human life might be like in a preferred future. As the phrase "think global, act local" has characterized futurist efforts to involve people where "they're at" (that is, geographically and socially), feminists might include the human element in the phrase "think futuristically, act daily," giving the movement a different kind of time dimension, making it more relevant to the present and the personal.

Feminists also see the task of future building as preserving and nurturing the positive elements and small-scale changes we all perceive and participate in. A positive future most likely will be made up of these elements of the preferred present that reflect the requisite values, behaviors, and world view changes that will constitute the larger transformation. Because of their more intimate physical connection to the life cycle, women understand that the future is not an abstract condition in a remote time. It is the process of becoming. Women know in their bones that the achievement of a preferred future requires us to act in the present on the basis of the norms and values we enshrine in our visions of transformation (Reardon, 1980).

As individual human development is cyclical, and often regresses at stages rather than progresses, so too a feminist view of transition is not a step-by-step linear progression but rather an organic, flowing and eddying notion of change. It is, I believe, this very notion of organic change with its expectation and understanding of recurrent regression that keeps women from despairing of their failures and infuses their continued struggle for a better life and for peace. I am, in fact, convinced that linear, step-by-step concepts of transition not only are bound to lead to severe disappointments, but are more likely to result in the despair that engulfs so many as the militarist negative trends increase in volume and speed.

Most women spend their efforts in areas for change where they can see the results. They work to change the particular circumstances in their local, daily environments and to change personal and social relationships; feminists add to this effort that of changing themselves. They make connections, both analytic and actual, among and between behaviors and consequences and most especially among and between individual persons. Their lives are made up of connections and linkages, circumstances affecting their visions of the future and their behaviors and decisions in the present. These feminine behaviors also reinforce the hypothesis of connection between personal change and structural change.

Another important, more recent reinforcement of this hypothesis is the validation of the assumption about the relationship between emotional maturity and positive social transformation to be found in Carol Gilligan's *In a Different Voice: Psychological Theory and Women's Development* (1982). Gilligan's work demonstrates a significant difference in the moral decision-making processes of men and women. She indicates contrasts not only in masculine and feminine ethical priorities and in the process of moral development and emotional maturation but even in modes of thinking. For the purposes of this inquiry into the connections between sexism and the war system, perhaps the most significant conclusion of her work is the potential contribution of feminine modes of thought to dealing constructively with the major global crises of security, justice, and equity in an interdependent world. Women's morality, she tells us, emerges from a concern with the human consequences of choices and actions.

> In a world that extends through an elaborate network of relationships, the fact that someone is hurt affects everyone who is involved, complicating the morality of any decision and removing the possibility of a clear or simple solution. Thus, morality, rather than being opposed to integrity or tied to an ideal of agreement, is aligned with the "kind of integrity" that comes from "making decisions after working through everything you think is involved and important in the situation," and taking responsibility for choice. In the end, morality is a matter of care. (Gilligan, 1982, p. 147)

In recounting women's development to moral maturity, Gilligan helps us to understand that full maturity for women involves two crucial elements: their acceptance of themselves as adult persons endowed with rights and the capacity to choose; and their development of the ability to comprehend both masculine abstract notions of justice and feminine contextual notions of care in their choice making. It thus becomes clear that justice and care are not exclusive but complementary moral concepts, and that both masculine and feminine modes have relevance to both public (political) and private (personal) choices. Most importantly, Gilligan's work illuminates the concept of maturity as the convergence of the two modes and thus provides us with a significant insight into the major intellectual and emotional components of transformation.

Not the least of these components is self-knowledge and self-acceptance. Painfully achieved by women, such knowledge is commonly avoided by men. As noted, the expectations and judgments society places on men are exacting, and it is likely that fear of not being able to stand up to judgment accounts for this avoidance. Thus men can continue to harbor notions that they are fundamentally peace loving and that they resort to violence primarily in the name of order and justice. This notion is damaging enough in the minds of men in general, but absolutely disastrous in stubborn world leaders in whom more self-knowledge could well mean a greater chance for human survival. Such leaders sharply exemplify the connection between the personal and the political as they guide human destiny from a dangerously individualistic, one-sided decision-making process, displaying little or no capacity to change. Both characteristics are paramount marks of immaturity.

Better self-understanding and authentic maturity will help us to see ourselves, our limitations, our possibilities, and our place in the larger order in such a light as to make us more capable of changing that order as we change the way we live our daily lives.

Masculine Mode, Feminine Mode: Separation and Connection

Gilligan (1982) points out how a masculine bias in the study of the different development emphases between men and women — men striving for separation and independence and women for connection and interdependence — has given us an unbalanced and inadequate notion of maturity. And, I would add, it has led to an overemphasis on individualism and the power to control, which so characterize the present dangerous stage of the war system, the arms race. These observations help us to see how the masculine bias actually has limited the conceptual repertoire and styles of problem resolution we bring to the arenas of politics and conflict. Individuation and separation have so determined our concepts of national interests that we are blinded to the many realities of interdependence that are the major determinants of our present world situation. That we are willing to risk our very survival to defend the national interest is not so surprising in a masculine-biased system when we understand that "the morality of rights differs from the morality of responsibility in its emphasis on separation rather than connection, in its consideration of the individual rather than the relationship as primary" (Gilligan, 1982, p. 19).

This significant difference in the types of morality that are developed by men and women provides us with an important insight into the causes of our present crises. It also suggests that transformation, the realization of global change, and transition, the process of achieving it, may well depend on the integration of masculine and feminine perspectives and modes in the processes of designing new structures and the political and educational programs to achieve them.

Finally, it seems to me, Gilligan's work lends further support to the hypothesis of reciprocal causation and provides grounds for the assertion that the structures of violence that constitute the war system are as much imbedded in the human psyche as in social structure. They are undoubtedly influenced by the attributes we use to guide the development of masculine identity and by masculine modes of public decision making. These factors are revealed only when the whole truth about the human experience is no longer filtered through an exclusive masculine bias, for "in the different voice of women lies the truth of an ethic of care, the tie between relationships and responsibility and the origins of aggression in the failure of connection" (Gilligan, 1982, p. 173).

More than any other scholar Gilligan gives us a fundamental understanding of the origins of masculine bias and how it has come to determine both social reality and our ways of interpreting and manipulating it. If we are to move away from these limited habits of mind, we must consider carefully the differences between the masculine and feminine modes of thought, which in turn are responsible for some of the significant differences between feminist scholarship and peace and world order studies.

The masculine mode approaches transformation and transition of the global order in the same analytic abstract fashion as it approaches other intellectual issues. The two concepts are perceived as a discrete set of end circumstances and a specific sequence of strategies to achieve them. The transformation, the end circumstances, generally are described in terms of *specific* structures and processes. These very often take the form of models that frequently appear to feminist and Third World eyes to be a rearrangement of traditional forms of power rather than a full and authentic transformation of the present reality.

Masculine models of transformation, frequently referred to as "system change," tend to be abstracted from everyday human conditions, to display a central concern with power arrangements, and to be preoccupied with the concept of sovereignty, an essentially patriarchal notion. Some focus much attention on determining which component of the revised structures will be endowed with the power and the right legitimately to use force, whether that force be armed or "nonviolent." Such models can be depicted by charts, diagrams, computer games, and institutional descriptions, but almost never do they have any explicit element of human relations or affective, emotional content, and few have displayed any cultural dimension.

The strategies set forth in the masculine mode for the transition process tend to be primarily political and economic. They are at their best in proposals for staged disarmament and plans for industrial conversion. They are conceived as steps to be taken in the public arena in a particular, incremental style (though of varying degrees of rapidity) and impacting primarily on public life. The value changes included in transition scenarios tend to be norms for social and public policies such as protection for human rights and procedures for conflict resolution. They are corporate rather than personal and conceived so as to have a direct impact on the public domain. The consequent effects of value changes on the private and personal spheres are given little if any more attention in world order transition strategies than in present public policy formation. This blindness to "secondary" consequences gives feminists, who do assess policy impact on women, cause for concern that the proposals are indeed more rearrangement than transformation. Indeed, it is this masculine preoccupation with the public and structural that has aborted the transformative potential of most twentieth-century revolutions. It kept them as just that: a revolution, a turning of the major power wheels that failed to produce changes in the fundamental global order. Such changes remove a particular group from political power but do not make connections to changes in the interpersonal realm nor to the nonmaterial sources of personal empowerment that feminism emphasizes. (It must be noted that some women researchers and futurists, myself included, have produced these same kinds of masculine scenarios.) The transition scenarios in the masculine mode have always been far weaker, less convincing, and less relevant either to the goal or the present reality than are their visions of transformed structures. In general there is a significant disjuncture between the transformative visions and the plans for the process to achieve them. Masculine models of transformation exhibit little or no consideration of the personal and individual changes that will be required. It is my opinion that this weakness in world order modeling results from the lack of the human, explicit, behavioral elements that are characteristic of the feminine mode.

The feminine mode, although weak in structuralism, is more developed in its approach to transition scenarios. Indeed the transition and the transformation in the feminine mode merge, and generally are viewed as one ecologically conceived, continuous, holistic process. There are few explicit feminist "relevant utopias," but there are feminist utopias. However, feminist, feminine, and women's images of the transformation are less precise in structural detail and public policy proposals.

Many of our feminine images of transformation are stories of personal and individual changes converged into social movements. The human dimension of both personal and social life is seen as a component of the same general complex of relations. Specific images are more weblike than structural. So, too, is women's view of life and human relations. The lack of distinct division between the transition and transformation is reflected in the way women envision the human experience. Take, for example, the adulthood of their children. This is seen not as a termination or culmination, but rather as the continuation of the development process, the living out of the values and world views that the family provides to them in their infancy and childhood. Feminine visions of transformation are less precise and abstract, more organic and behavioral than are masculine visions. The images tend to be of convergence, healing, wholeness, birth, and new life.

Feminine images are contextual and more concerned with textures, feelings, and relationships than with public policy, economic process, or political structure, although those elements are not entirely excluded. They are often centered on the emergence of self-awareness and the development of self-reliance and responsibility in the contexts of mutuality and equity. They are frequently stories of coming of age, and very often involve personal change and human support systems that make such change possible. Feminist equivalents of world order transition strategies are the building of the support systems that are at once the ignition and the motor of the change process. Women have been very successful at risk assessment and survival assurance in undertaking both personal change and political action, particularly in their efforts in the peace movement. Indeed, the networking phenomena in the present global movement, in my opinion, are mainly the work of the women who have been playing key roles in organizing and strategizing. They seek in feminine fashion to make connections, to establish and nurture relationships. They share responsibility and authority and function without hierarchy. Indeed, many women's groups are practicing models of structural transformation. Feminine concepts of transition are views of the maturing of a society moving from competition, alienation, and fragmentation to cooperation, complementarity, and integration. A feminine "language of responsibilities provides a web-like image of relationships to replace a hierarchical ordering that dissolves with the coming of equality" (Gilligan, 1982, p. 173).

Because these images and feminine approaches have had little consideration in the general literature or academic or political discussions of future world orders, there is insufficient attention to the fact that feminine visions do provide a viable alternative to the rearrangements of hierarchical structures that so preoccupy masculine visions.

Most feminist visions or models of the future world order are found not in academic essays, computerized games, graphs, or charts but in novels, poetry, works of art, and specific behavioral changes that women are currently making in themselves and seeking to help others to make. Women are significantly active in initiating political movements, particularly movements related to peace and justice, but they have yet to be as concerned with political strategy design and the devising of structural changes for the institutionalization of the kind of human interrelationships they seek. Yet their current efforts and their visions of healing and wholeness are in some ways far more transformative than the precise structural designs and abstract political processes that male researchers have offered to date.

Transcending Polarization:
Reconciliation as a World Order Value

To move toward a broader comprehension of the meaning of healing and wholeness in our fragmented world and to comprehend the full dimensions of the transformational task, we need to take note of the many damaging divisions and separations that are in large part a consequence of the masculine bias in science, politics, and social structures in general. We need to focus on the major separations and dichotomies in thought and social functions and the consequent inequity, conflict, and violence that this bias has produced. Among the deepest of these divisions that the feminine flow toward healing and wholeness call us to transcend are those between science and philosophy, fact and value, the individual and the community, the family and the state, the public and the private spheres, citizens and nurturers, and male and female social roles. For example, citizenship in a feminist future order would carry responsibility to nurture and enhance life as well as participate in politics and public affairs. Nurturing and political activities would be the common concern of both men and women. What a different politics that would make!

Even our ways of identifying and becoming ourselves and of mediating the human experience must be transformed to overcome separations and dichotomies. I do not advocate merger into a homogeneous culture or uniform human identity, but rather, a transcendence of the abstract, dichotomous thinking that impedes the flourishing of the myriad ways of being human. Such thinking has produced a we-they syndrome, which divides and factionalizes the world along the lines of economic wealth and systems, geopolitical positions, and ideology and culture. The worth of other systems and cultures is judged by the degree of their similarity to those judging. We think in large, dichotomous, dangerously obscuring terms, such as the West and the non-West, developed and developing, socialist and capitalist. It is this dichotomous, competitive, polarizing thinking that has negatively exaggerated and manipulated the differences between men and women and kept us playing the war game for most of human history.

This lethal game has enabled us to make sharp, often spurious distinctions between good and evil and led us to make our own kind, if not ourselves, the personification of virtue and symbols of the highest human attainment, ascribing to the other images of corruption and lesser accomplishments. It has also exaggerated the differences of otherness, making it the precondition to becoming the enemy. Only now, as the weapons and strategies we have created to play this monstrous game threaten to annihilate us as we "defend ourselves against the enemy," do we begin to understand the profound truth of Pogo's declaration that "We have met the enemy and he is us!" Herein lies the answer to the problems both of our maturation and of our survival.

There is no human being on earth who is not other to most of the human species. We are amazingly and marvelously varied for one single species. And single species we are, with one future or none. The real enemy of humanity is the failure to recognize and act on this truth. The realization of our common destiny needs to be taken into consideration at all levels of human choice and human behavior, not only at the level of nuclear policy. We must acknowledge, as Robert Lifton says, "If you die, I die. If you survive, I survive," but also, and perhaps more basically, "If you are debased, I am debased. If your identity is distorted, so is mine." The survival and progress of the human species does not depend on it universally adopting the masculine model of modernization as the mode of development. The equality of women does not depend on their accepting masculine values and behaviors. Global security does not depend on all nations having parity of arms with their enemies. Neither our integrity nor our identity requires debasing the other or defeating the enemy.

Beyond the failure to acknowledge these truths, the only other authentic enemy is the fear of the other, which I believe is at base fear of our own weaknesses and shortcomings — which we suspect to be the other in us. What I am advocating here is a new world order value, reconciliation, and perhaps even forgiveness, not only of those who trespass against us, but primarily of ourselves. By understanding that no human being is totally incapable of the most reprehensible of human acts, or of the most selfless and noble, we open up the possibilities for change of cosmic dimensions. Essentially this realization is what lies at the base of the philosophy of nonviolence. If we are to move through a disarmed world to a truly nonviolent one, to authentic peace and justice, we must come to terms with and accept the other in ourselves, be it our masculine or our feminine attributes or any of those traits and characteristics we have projected on enemies and criminals, or heroes and saints.

If we advocate the equal value and dignity of all persons, we need also accept their shortcomings as well as their gifts and talents, and understand that all (even ourselves) are capable of changing. The question is whether we will be motivated to do so. My own belief is that this motivation is primarily a task for education, particularly for peace education. Indeed, we have seen little evidence of motivation to change either in the bastions of male chauvinism or in the entrenched militaristic social system. But without the possibility of such change there is little hope of escaping from the war system trap. Education is an enterprise based on hope and the possibility of change.

At its best, education, like the struggle for peace, is motivated by love. The facts that men and women continue to love each other, and that some even struggle to understand each other despite the overwhelming dimensions of the system that separates and alienates us from each other, are a tremendous source of hope. So, too, is the growing bonding among women transcending a socialization that separated and alienated them from each other, setting them into competition to win the favor of men. As men have bonded in the hunt and on the battlefields and playing fields, women now bond in the feminist movement and in the peace movement, offering each other some of the love and support they have been socialized to lavish on husbands and children. They are supporting and nurturing each other through personal change and political challenge. Such sources of hope make it possible to believe we can change. It is this belief that feminists find empowering and from which we take a new definition of *power*: the capacity to change, to change ourselves and our environment.

Indeed, the empowerment of the powerless is the fundamental change required to transcend sexism and the war system. It would be the very antithesis of the present coercive use of power. It is one of the major motivations behind the feminist demand that women have control over their own bodies, the prime requisite of empowerment, and it clearly makes these women's issues world order issues. It means as well that world order must at last fully embrace that elusive fifth value, *participation*, as it moves toward the stronger, more transformative value of universal human empowerment. Only through this kind of process can we be liberated from the continued global dominance of the industrial male elites. Women's movements, anticolonial movements, and all forms of human rights movements are evidence that such a process is underway. All such movements begin with the refusal of the oppressed to continue to accept their inferior status as inevitable or deserved. Value of self, a primary value of feminism, is essential to the process of liberation and to the development of mature responsibility. As Gilligan observes about this process in women:

> Release from the intimidation of inequality finally allows women to express a judgment that had previously been withheld. . . . The willingness to express and to take responsibility for judgment stems from a recognition of the psychological costs of indirect action, to self and to other and thus to relationships. Responsibility for care then includes both self and other and the injunction not to hurt, freed from conventional constraints sustains the ideal of care while focusing the reality of choice. (1982, p. 95)

The most significant aspect of the process is recognizing the costs. Empowerment, self-respect, and authentic responsibility are not easily come by, not by individuals or societies. Nor do we have the specific strategies of empowerment at hand. However, given the commitment and the visions, feminist strategies are born out of specific contexts and conditions. For example, the Women's Pentagon Action and the Greenham Common and Seneca Falls encampments could not have been projected as transition strategies in advance of the specific policies they responded to. These actions are examples, too, of risk, sacrifice, and painful — but joyous — struggle. And, like birth itself, the joy in the labor comes from a vision of a new life and of life renewed. The actions required an inner struggle, a change in self, and learning to deal with the profound difficulties of applying new principles to personal and daily life. They are, indeed, examples of the interrelationship between the cosmic and the quotidian.

These examples hold forth the possibility of relating to others, and to the other, as full persons, not as enemies or objects. The focus was on both political objective, or social model, and on human relations. They seemed to combine the masculine abstract intellectual approach with the feminine concrete, practical approach. This, it seems to me, is what we need in transition strategies — a convergence of masculine and feminine styles of change.

There is a significant similarity between feminist peace strategists and male practitioners of nonviolence in their refusal to accede to the seemingly unchangeable, and their challenge to the authority of raw, coercive power. They have taken responsibility to ask the fundamental questions about the necessity of human suffering. Questioning, taking responsibility, empowerment and value of self are attributes of maturity and transformation. They are evidence, too, of the convergence of positive masculine and feminine values, modes of thought, and styles of action. These developments are cited as signs of the hoped-for convergence of feminism and the peace movement, and to indicate that the possibilities for truly transformatory movements can be greatly enhanced by encouraging and widening this convergence. The possibility of a cultural transformation of unprecedented proportions is, indeed, emerging. The chances of making that possibility become a probability, of achieving a truly human future, will be enhanced by deeper study of the connections between sexism and the war system. The potential for transformation that I see in the knowledge such study would yield gives me hope at a time when ordinary politics and traditional scholarship offer none.

Conclusion:
Reproducing the Future

Because one major purpose of this monograph has been to reflect on the life-enhancing possibilities of feminism and women's movements, the language of human reproduction provides an appropriate frame for the conclusion. The conception of a transformed society will be found in the actualizing of the central ideas that will give birth to that society. As male and female genetic material converge in the conception of an individual human life, so must masculine and feminine perceptions, modes, and participation merge into a conception of a truly human society. This conception can be politically symbolized by taking on as one goal the two major transformative tasks of our generation: achieving equality for women and complete disarmament. Achieving the first task would give social value to positive feminine human traits, and the accomplishment of the second would require denial of social value to the most negative masculine traits.

The gestation of the transformed society would be in the processes we devise to develop the basic conception into a living social order, capable of maturing into an entity no longer dependent on specific structures or controlled by the circumstances that led to its conception. Such processes are likely to be simultaneous and complementary behavioral and structural changes guided by the masculine values of justice and equality and the feminine values of care and equity. Transition strategies equal to this task can be designed only by men and women together working in a style of true mutuality.

The "cry of life" of the transformation might be the public articulation and institutionalization of the fundamental values derived from the parents. The birth would be symbolized, as have been the births of societies for centuries, by the inauguration of new governing structures. Such an inauguration might be the formal recognition of the institutional framework of a global peace system, derived as the result of the equal political participation of men and women in the maintenance and development of a disarmed and demilitarized world.

The maturity of such a peace system would be indicated by continuous reflection on and challenge to its rules and structures and by its capacity to change in response to new conditions leading to new stages of human maturation. Maturity is, in the last analysis, the capacity to transform, and to bring forth new life. Transformation is the continuous process by which human beings exercise choice, change reality, and find meaning. Transformation is life. Feminism chooses life.

REFERENCES
INDEX
ABOUT THE AUTHOR

REFERENCES

Anonymous. (1967). *A report from Iron Mountain*. New York: Dial Press.

Bengis, I. (1972). *Combat in the erogenous zones*. New York: Random House.

Boulding, E. (1981). *Perspectives of women researchers on disarmament, national security, and world order*. Prepublication draft.

Brock-Utne, B. (1981). *The role of women as mothers and as members of society in the education of young people for peace, mutual understanding, and peace* (Publication S-12/81). Oslo, Norway: Peace Research Institute of Oslo.

Brownmiller, S. (1976). *Against our will: Men, women, and rape*. New York: Bantam.

Burns, R. (1982, March). *Development, disarmament, and women: Some new connections*. Paper presented at the Victorian Association for Peace Studies, Melbourne, Australia.

Carroll, B. (1972). Peace research: The cult of power. *Conflict Resolution, 16*(4), 585–616.

Chilchinisky, G. (1978, October). *Women's exclusion from mathematics and science*. Paper presented at the International Symposium on Women's Political Participation, Berkeley, CA.

Chodorow, N. (1978). *The reproduction of mothering: Psychoanalysis and the sociology of gender*. Berkeley, CA: University of California Press.

COPRED [Consortium on Peace Research, Education and Development]. (1978a). *Conclusion and evaluation* [Organizer's report on the International Symposium on Women's Political Participation]. Kent, OH: Author.

COPRED [Consortium on Peace Research, Education and Development]. (1978b). *Report from the third world group* [Organizer's report on the International Symposium on Women's Political Participation]. Kent, OH: Author.

Crahan, M. (1982). *Human rights and basic needs in the Americas*. Washington, DC: Georgetown University Press.

Divale, W. T., & Harris, M. (1976). Population, warfare, and the male supremacist complex. *American Anthropologist, 78*, 521–533.

Elster, E. (1981). Patriarchy. In *Loaded Questions*. Washington, DC: Institute for Policy Studies.

Enloe, C. (1981). The military model. In *Loaded Questions*. Washington, DC: Institute for Policy Studies.

Falk, R. (1980). *A world order perspective on authoritarian tendencies* (Working Paper #10). New York: World Policy Institute [Formerly Institute for World Order].

Falk, R. (1981). *Normative initiatives and demilitarization: A third system approach* (Working Paper #13). New York: World Policy Institute [Formerly Institute for World Order].

Feigen-Fasteau, M. (1978). *The male machine.* New York: Delta Books.

Fitzgerald, F. (1980, February 17). *New York Times,* sec. 4, p. 19, col. 1.

Fornari, F. (1974). *The psychoanalysis of war* (A. Pfeifer, Trans.). New York: Anchor Press.

Forsberg, R. (1982, Fall). A nuclear freeze and a non-interventionary conventional policy. *Teachers College Record, 84*(1), 65–78.

French, M. (1981). *The bleeding heart.* New York: Random House.

Galtung, J. (1980). *Peace and world structure* (Essays in Peace Research Series, No. 4). Copenhagen, Denmark: Christian Ejlers.

Garcia Chafardet, I. (1975). Proposal for a doctoral dissertation presented to the Department of Political Science, New York University.

Garcia Chafardet, I. (1978, October). *Sexism and a proposed theory of aggression.* Paper presented at the International Symposium on Women's Political Participation, Berkeley, CA.

Gilligan, C. (1982). *In a different voice: Psychological theory and women's development.* Cambridge, MA: Harvard University Press.

Greer, G. (1971). *The female eunuch.* New York: McGraw-Hill.

Heide, W. S. (1980, June). Testimony for the record and inclusion in the *Final report to the President and Congress* from the U.S. Commission on Proposals for a National Academy of Peace and Conflict Resolution, Washington, DC.

Henderson, H. (1978). *Creating alternative futures: The end of economics.* New York: Berkley Publishing.

ILO [International Labor Organization]. *Women at work* [Monograph series, 8 issues annually]. Geneva, Switzerland: Author.

International Tribunal on Crimes Against Women. (1976). *Final report.* Brussels, Belgium: Author.

Johansen, R. (1978a). *Salt II: Illusion and reality* (Working Paper #9). New York: World Policy Institute [Formerly Institute for World Order].

Johansen, R. (1978b). *Toward a dependable peace* (Working Paper #8). New York: World Policy Institute [Formerly Institute for World Order].

Kelber, M. (1982). *Women and the arms race.* Lecture presented at Barnard College, Columbia University, New York.

Kohler, G. (1979). *Global apartheid* (Working Paper #7). New York: World Policy Institute [Formerly Institute for World Order].

Konner, M. (1982). He and she. *Science, 3*(7).

Land, P. (1982). On human work. *Center Focus, 49*, 3–4.

Lasch, C. (1979). *The culture of narcissism*. New York: Norton.

Lee, P., & Gropper, N. (1974). Sex-role, culture, and educational practice. *Harvard Educational Review, 44*(3), 369–410.

Lifton, R., & Falk, R. (1982). *Indefensible weapons*. New York: Basic Books.

McSorley, R. (1982). *Kill? for peace* (2d rev. ed.). Washington, DC: Georgetown University, Center for Peace Studies.

Mallmann, C. (1978, October). Assertion made in opening plenary discussion at the International Symposium on Women's Political Participation, Berkeley, CA.

Mazrui, A. (1974). Untitled paper presented at a meeting of the World Order Models Project, Northampton, MA.

Melman, S. (1974). *The permanent war economy*. New York: Simon & Schuster.

New Abolitionists, The. (1978). Proceedings of the Riverside Church Disarmament Conference, New York.

Oberg, J. (1981). The new international military order, the real threat to human security: An essay on global armaments, structural militarism, and alternative security. *University of Oslo Chair in Conflict Resolution Papers, 65*. Oslo, Norway: University of Oslo.

Papa, M. B. (1981, April 24). Violence, like church, "keeps women in line." *The National Catholic Reporter*, p. 33.

Reardon, B. (1975a). Comments on the State of the Globe Message. *Alternatives, 1*(4), 561–565.

Reardon, B. (1975b). [Editorial on UN Conference on International Women's Year]. *Earthrise* [Out of print].

Reardon, B. (1975c). Women's movements and human futures. *Convergence, 8*(3), 41–52.

Reardon, B. (1977a). *Discrimination: The cycle of injustice*. Sidney, Australia: Holt Saunders.

Reardon, B. (1977b). Women and structural violence: A crucial issue for peace education. *Peace Education, 1*(1), 19–27.

Reardon, B. (1980, January/February). Moving to the future. *Network, 8*(1), 14–21.

Reardon, B. (1981, Fall). Militarism and sexism: Influences on education for war. *Connexion, 9*(3), 6–10.

Reardon, B. (1984). *A gender analysis of militarization*. Unpublished manuscript.

Rivers, C. (1982, August 29). ERA's death and the fear of new women. *New York Times*, sec. 4, p. 19.

Roberts, B. (1982, August). *Peace studies and the war against women: A survey of research*. Paper presented at a meeting of the Canadian Peace Research Association, Toronto.

Roberts, W. (Producer/Director). (1980). *Between men* [Film]. Franklin Lakes, NJ: United Documentary.

Sakamoto, Y. (1981, June). *Report of the Secretary General*. Presented to the General Conference of the International Peace Research Association, Orilla, Canada.

Siskel, G. (1981–82). *Sneak previews* [Film reviews telecast over WNET].

Sivard, R. (Ed.). (1982). *World military and social expenditures*. Washington, DC: World Priorities, Inc.

Sivard, R. (Ed.). (1983). *World military and social expenditures*. Washington, DC: World Priorities, Inc.

Sloan, D. (1983). *Insight-imagination: The emancipation of thought and the modern world*. Westport, CT: Greenwood Press.

Stanford, B. (1981, June). *The human capacity for disarmament: A preliminary survey of biological, psychological, and anthropological surveys*. Paper presented at the General Conference of the International Peace Research Association, Orilla, Canada.

Stiehm, J. (1979, August). *Women and citizenship: Mobilization, participation, representation*. Paper presented at the International Political Science Association, Moscow.

Talese, G. (1980). *Thy neighbor's wife*. New York: Dell Books.

Thurman, J. (1982, September). [Interview with Nancy Chodorow]. *Ms. Magazine*, p. 138.

Wolpin, M. (1981). *Women as combatants, implications for sexism and militarism*. Preliminary research proposal.

Women's Pentagon Action. (1980). *Women's Pentagon Action Statement*. New York: Author.

Zanotti, B. (1979, October). *Militarism and violence: A feminist perspective*. Paper presented at the Riverside Church Disarmament Conference, New York.

INDEX

Academia, 78–79

African Women's Association for Research Development, 82

Against Our Will (Brownmiller), 40

Aggression
  causes of, 8, 41–43, 53
  as conscious choice, 43
  men conditioned for, 37–38, 42
  society's cultivation of, 20

Anatomy of Freedom, The (Morgan), 85n

Apartheid system, global, 75–76

Arms race. *See also* Disarmament
  causes of, 14, 27
  as peace barrier, 34–35
  psychological perspectives on, 77–78
  repressive purpose of, 46
  sexism linked to, 46
  sex-role stereotypes supportive of, 58–59
  structural violence and, 60–61
  women's concern with, 58–63

Authoritarianism
  behaviors conditioned by, 38
  caring and, 30–31
  social justice ignored by, 30–31
  war system and, 10, 12
  women's status and, 75

Balch, Emily Greene, 64

Bataille, Georges, 27

Bengis, I., 51

Between Men (Roberts), 53

Bleeding Heart, The (French), 50

Bocaccio, Ann, 61

Boulding, E., 73

Brock-Utne, Birgit, 33, 58, 64, 79

Brownmiller, S., 39–40, 47, 69–70

Burns, Robin, 60–61

Caldicott, Helen, 72

Campaign for Nuclear Disarmament, 72

Capitalist imperialism, 67–68

Carroll, Berenice, 65, 81

Castration anxiety, 34–35

Chilchinisky, G., 14

Child abuse, 45, 54

Chivalry, 53–54

Chodorow, Nancy, 52, 68

Coffin, William Sloane, 51

Colonialism, 60

Columbia University Human Rights Center, 62

Combat in the Erogenous Zones (Bengis), 51

Communication gaps
  between sexes, 48–50
  in disarmament movement, 49
  patriarchy served by, 49–50

Consortium on Peace Research, Education and Development (COPRED), 67–68

Copernicus, Nicolaus, 13

Decision making
  feminine modes of, 87
  masculine modes of, 89

Dedring, Juergen, 65

Disarmament. *See also* Arms race
  castration anxiety and, 34
  fear inhibitory to, 6, 8
  sexism inhibitory to, 4

ABOUT THE AUTHOR

BETTY REARDON, director of the United Ministries in Education's Peacemaking in Education Program, also serves as coordinator of the Peace Education Program of Teachers College, Columbia University. Active for many years in the development of peace education, she was one of the founders of the Peace Education Commission of the International Peace Research Association and has done extensive consulting with various international and national organizations and educational institutions. Her writings on peace education, disarmament education, human rights, and women's issues have been widely published in the United States and abroad.